Computerized Accounting
Using
Great Plains *Dynamics*

First Edition

1999

INSTRUCTIONS
AND
ASSIGNMENTS

By

Alvin A. Arens
D. Dewey Ward

Professors of Accounting
Michigan State University

ISBN 0-912503-13-0

Printed in the United States of America

Acknowledgements

Completing *Computerized Accounting Using Great Plains Dynamics* required considerable coordination and cooperation between the authors and Great Plains personnel. We were impressed with their commitment to help us develop educational material that will help future accountants learn computerized accounting, their flexibility in allowing us to keep every aspect of the project as simple as practical, and their assistance in marketing the project to educators. We are especially grateful for their granting us permission to provide Great Plains *Dynamics* software. We specifically acknowledge the following individuals for their helpfulness: **Kristin Anderson**, **Cathy Green**, **Cheri Schoenfish**, and **Lee Spiesman**.

Carol Borsum has been a practicing CPA and is now an experienced and competent reviewer, editor, and writer of accounting textbook materials. She has been a major contributor to every aspect of this project. These materials would not have been completed without her contributions.

Mary Jo Mercer has word processed too many drafts of these materials to count. Her dedication, competence, and perseverance are greatly appreciated.

Alvin A. Arens
D. Dewey Ward

Table of Contents

CHAPTER 1

Introduction and
Software Installation

Welcome to learning *Great Plains Dynamics*. You will be using these materials to learn how to use a sophisticated accounting package by following a carefully designed approach.

Materials Included in the Package

The materials that you have purchased are made up of four items:

- **CD.** The CD includes *Dynamics'* programs and all company information needed to complete the project.

- **Instructions and Assignments Book.** This book is the starting point for all assignments. It will guide you through *Dynamics*. Unless your course instructor informs you otherwise, **you should start with Chapter 1 and proceed through the materials without skipping any parts**.

- **Reference Book.** The Reference book provides instructions for using each of the windows discussed in these materials. You will be referring to the Reference book frequently in later chapters. You will be instructed when to use the Reference book as you go through the Instructions and Assignments book.

- **Reference Summary Card.** The laminated Reference Summary Card is designed to help you locate the appropriate pages in the Reference book for recording transactions or doing other activities.

System Requirements

The minimum hardware requirements for running the *Great Plains Dynamics Student Version* software include a Pentium 90 computer, 200 MB of available hard disk space, a CD-ROM drive, and 32 MB of RAM. Operating system requirements include Windows 98, Windows 95, or Windows NT Workstation 4.0.

Troubleshooting

Instructions for correcting errors are located in Appendix A of the Reference book. In addition, *Dynamics* has an extensive Help menu you can use to learn more about specific windows and functions within the program. The Help menu is discussed more fully in Chapter 2.

Very rarely, *Dynamics* may display an error message when you try to start the program or open a specific company. This problem usually occurs when you exited the Dynamics program improperly during the previous session. An example of when this situation may occur is when there is a power failure and your computer shuts down while you are using the *Dynamics* program. The error message will typically indicate that your User ID is already logged onto the system or that it is not allowed to enter the system. If you get locked out of the program, complete the following steps:

🖳 *Click the Cancel button in the Users and Companies window if this window is open.*

🖳 *Open Windows Explorer.*

🖳 *Locate the Dynstdt folder on the left half of the window. Open the System folder within the Dynstdt folder.*

🖳 *Delete the following two files shown in the right half of the window: ACTIVITY.dat and ACTIVITY.idx.* **Be careful to delete only these two files. Deleting any other files may cause the entire *Dynamics* program to crash.**

🖳 *Close Windows Explorer.*

🖳 *Open the Dynamics program again to continue your work.*

Additional Diskettes Needed for Students Doing the Project in a Computer Laboratory (Optional for all other Students)

If you are doing the project in a computer laboratory, you will need to purchase *two blank diskettes* for saving the data that you process. You should purchase these diskettes before proceeding. You are strongly encouraged to use new diskettes, not ones previously used.

If you are using your own computer for the project, you can do the project without diskettes. However, if you are concerned with data loss on your hard drive and you want to back up your data externally, you will need two blank diskettes also.

Introduction

The purposes of accounting software are to keep accounting records accurately and efficiently and provide relevant financial information to management and other users. One type of financial information needed by users is periodic financial statements, but there are many other types of information used primarily by management, such as aged trial balances, sales reports by sales person and product, inventory quantities on hand, and property, plant and equipment details.

Three important characteristics of accounting software are (1) its ability to generate multiple-use information without entering information more than once, (2) the incorporation of shortcut methods to enter data, and (3) the embedding of internal controls in the software to detect and prevent errors. There are hundreds of examples of all three in most accounting software. An example of the first is the automatic update of sales and receivable reports, the master file of accounts receivable, sales journal, general ledger, and inventory and accounts receivable master files when a sales invoice is prepared. An example of the second is the automatic inclusion of a customer's name and address when the customer's identification number is entered in the system. An example of the third is the rejection of an accounting transaction where relevant information, such as the customer's name, is not entered for a transaction.

There is a wide variety of accounting software available for companies to purchase and modify for their company's needs. Examples of accounting software for small companies are *Peachtree Complete Accounting*, *MYOB*, and *QuickBooks*. The software used in this project, *Great Plains Dynamics*, was developed by Great Plains Software, Inc. of Fargo, North Dakota. This package is widely used by larger businesses and is commercially available from Great Plains. *Dynamics* is intended for medium-size and larger companies, but would probably not be appropriate for a Fortune 1000 company. The reason for selecting *Dynamics* for this project is the relative ease of using the program, while including some of the sophistication of more complex software.

An important characteristic of *Dynamics* is the ability to modify the software to deal with small businesses or more complex ones. The authors have simplified the software to the degree practical without eliminating its essential features.

Key Activities Included in the Project

Accountants perform several types of activities when they use accounting software such as *Dynamics* to keep accounting records for companies. You will do many of these activities during the project. These activities are introduced in Chapters 1 and 2 and are dealt with more extensively in later assignments. Following are key activities you will be doing in the project:

- **Install the *Dynamics* software and back up data.** You will learn this in Chapter 1.

- **Enter the *Dynamics* program and a company.** You must be able to access *Dynamics* and the company for which you will be performing activities.

- **Enter transactions, including all information needed for recordkeeping.** Accountants spend most of their time recording transactions and this is the primary emphasis of the project. An example of recordkeeping for transactions is entering data to bill customers for shipped goods, preparing the sales invoice, and recording the sale and related accounts receivable, including updating subsidiary records for accounts receivable and inventory.

- **Inquire about recorded information.** Management and other employees of companies frequently need information about data in the system. For example, if a customer calls about an apparent incorrect billing, it is important to respond quickly. *Dynamics* provides access to data in a variety of ways to permit many different types of inquiries.

- **Review and print reports.** Users of accounting information need reports in a proper format with an adequate level of detail for their decision making. Examples include an aged trial balance for accounts receivable, an income statement and a report of sales by sales person or product. *Dynamics* permits many different reports to be prepared and printed, and allows tailoring to meet users' needs.

- **Do maintenance.** An important characteristic of accounting software is the automatic performance of many mechanical activities by the computer. To permit the computer to do these activities, maintenance is done to provide an adequate database of information. For example, *Dynamics* permits a user to enter a customer's identification number and the software will automatically include the customer's name and address on a sales invoice. In this example, maintenance is done to associate the customer name and address with the customer identification number.

Steps to Install, Back Up, Restore a Backup, and Uninstall *Dynamics*

For the entire project, the following symbol is used to indicate that you are to perform a step using your computer:

Whenever you see this symbol in the left margin, you should complete the related step, which is shown in italics. You should not begin doing an activity with your computer until the symbol is shown.

The procedures you will follow for installation, back up, restoring a backup, and uninstalling are different depending on whether you are using:

a. Your own computer and plan to keep the *Dynamics* software on your hard drive until you complete the project. If this is your situation, follow the four steps on pages 1-6 to 1-14.

b. A computer laboratory or other computer where you will most likely remove the *Dynamics* software each time you stop using the computer. If this is your situation, follow the five steps on pages 1-14 to 1-24.

Be sure to follow only the instructions that apply to your circumstances.

You Use your Own Computer and Plan to Keep the Dynamics Software On Your Hard Drive Until you Complete the Project

STEP 1. INSTALL THE *GREAT PLAINS DYNAMICS STUDENT VERSION SOFTWARE.* There are two methods for beginning the install process:

💻 *With the computer on, insert the program CD into your CD-ROM drive.* The setup window below should appear automatically in less than a minute.

If this method does not automatically start the setup process, do the following:

💻 *Make sure the program CD is in your CD-ROM drive. Click Start → Run. Type d:cdsetup.exe (where d: represents the drive letter of your CD-ROM drive). Click OK.* The setup window below will appear.

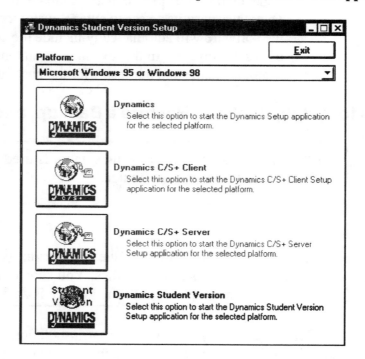

This is the first installation window. From this window you should:

🖥 *Verify the Platform at the top of the window.* An example of a platform is Microsoft Windows 95 or 98. The installation program will detect the platform that you are using, but you can change the default if needed. It is unlikely that you will need to change it.

🖥 *Click the Dynamics Student Version icon at the bottom of the window. If you are not ready to begin the installation, click Exit in the top right corner.*

Review the welcome and licensing information on the following screen:

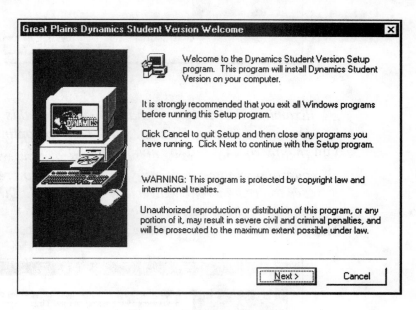

🖥 *Click Next to continue.* The following window appears:

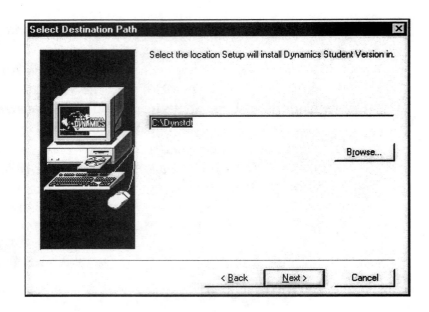

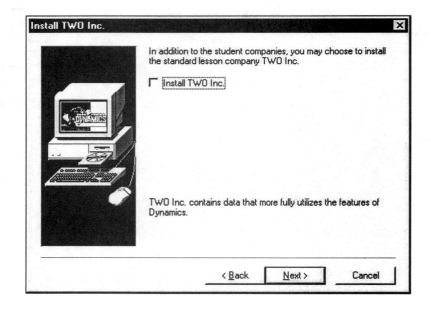

🖳 *Examine the directory that appears on this window to install the Dynamics Student Version. Click Next to continue.*

🖳 *If this directory has not been created, you will be prompted with a question window asking if you would like to create the directory. Click Yes to create the new directory if prompted. Otherwise, click Next.*

The following window appears:

⌨ *If you will be completing Chapter 5, which uses the sample company, The World Online (TWO Inc.), you should check the box to install TWO Inc. in the preceding window. This company takes an additional 30 megs of hard drive space to install.*

⌨ **Click the Install TWO Inc. box unless your instructor has informed you otherwise.** *No*

⌨ *Click Next to continue.*

The installation will include a *Great Plains Dynamics Student Version* option on your Start Program menu as shown on the following window.

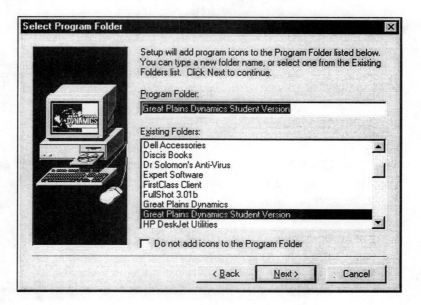

⌨ *You need not make any changes in the settings in this window. Click Next to continue.*

The following window appears and allows you to verify the settings that you chose during the installation process.

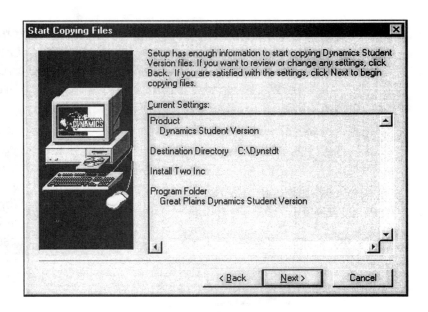

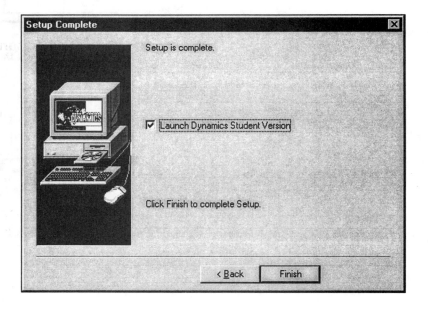

Click Next to continue.

    The setup software will begin copying *Great Plains Dynamics Student Version* files to your hard drive. Because there are a large number of files, installation may take several minutes.

    You have completed installing the *Great Plains Dynamics Student Version* when the following window appears.

⌨ *Assuming you plan to use the Great Plains Dynamics Student Version immediately, click Finish.* You will receive a Users and Companies Window like the one on page 2-3 (Chapter 2). After reviewing the information below for Steps 2 through 4, you are ready to begin Chapter 2.

⌨ *In the unlikely event that you would like to exit the program and use Dynamics at a later time, remove the check mark from the box in front of the words "Launch Dynamics Student Version" and then click Finish.*

Installation is now complete. The remaining pages through the middle of page 1-14 are for Steps 2 through 4. Each step is summarized below and on the top of the next page. You do not need to read the details of these steps on pages 1-11 to 1-14 now, **but note their content as described next because you will use them later**.

Step 2 on pages 1-11 to 1-13 — *Backup*. Use this step when you want to back up your data files. The first time this is likely is at the end of Chapter 3.

Step 3 on page 1-13 — *Restore a Backup*. Use this step when you want to restore company data that you have backed up previously. This can be useful if you want to start one of the chapters over again. This is most likely to happen when you are doing Chapter 4.

Step 4 on pages 1-13 and 1-14 — *Uninstall*. Refer to this step only when the entire project is complete and you want to remove all *Dynamics* software and related data files from your computer.

For later use, remember the location of these important steps. Refer back to them each time you need to perform one of the steps.

STEP 2. BACK UP YOUR DATA FILES TO AN INTERNAL LOCATION ON YOUR HARD DRIVE. It is not mandatory that you back up your data files because posted transactions are automatically saved in the Dynstdt folder on your hard drive. However, it is recommended that you back up the data files each time you complete a work session. You will need to use these backup files only if you wish to redo part of the project but not other parts. If you are concerned about possible loss of data on your hard drive and want to back up your data externally to diskettes, refer to Step 2 on pages 1-20 to 1-22 (Backup) and Step 5 on pages 1-23 and 1-24 (Restore).

Procedures to Back Up Data Files

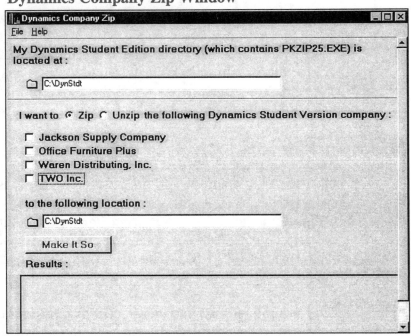

💻 *Exit the Dynamics program if it is open.*

💻 *Click Start → Programs → Great Plains Dynamics Student Version →*
Backup or Restore Dynamics Data. The following window opens:

Dynamics Company Zip Window

There are two radio buttons in this window: Zip (backup) and Unzip (restore).
Because the default is Zip, you do not have to do anything to these radio buttons
when backing up company data files.

The four companies used in this project are listed in the window and each
company has a blank check box next to it. The default location where the backups
will be saved is in the Dynstdt folder on your hard drive. A separate *.zip file will
be created for each company you back up.

💻 *Click the check box(es) to insert a check mark(s) next to the company
(companies) you want to back up. **Be sure to select the correct company
or companies.***

💻 *Click the "Make It So" box.*

The program will take several seconds to complete the backup process. When the process is done, the Results box will list what has been done.

⌨ *Close the Dynamics Company Zip window when the backup process is finished.*

STEP 3. RESTORE A BACKUP. If you decide to redo a portion of the project, you will restore your data files that you backed up in Step 2. If you have backed up previously to diskettes and want to restore the data files from the diskettes, refer to Step 5 on pages 1-23 and 1-24. It is unlikely that you will need to do Step 3.

Procedures to Restore a Backup

The *Dynamics* Company Zip window is also used to restore company data files from the backup files to the company data files in the *Dynamics* application program. To restore company data files, complete the following steps:

⌨ *Exit the Dynamics program if it is open.*
⌨ *Click Start → Programs → Great Plains Dynamics Student Version → Backup or Restore Dynamics Data to open the Dynamics Company Zip window.*
⌨ *Click the Unzip (restore) radio button.*
⌨ *Click the check box(es) to insert a check mark(s) next to the company (companies) you are restoring. Be sure to select the correct company or companies.*
⌨ *Check to make sure that the location in the "from the following location" box is the same place where you backed up the files earlier.*
⌨ *Click the "Make It So" button.*

The program will take several seconds to complete the restore process. When the process is done, the Results box will list what has been done.

⌨ *Close the Dynamics Company Zip window.*

STEP 4. UNINSTALL THE *GREAT PLAINS DYNAMICS STUDENT VERSION* SOFTWARE. When you have completely finished the project and have handed in all required assignments to your instructor, you can remove the *Great Plains Dynamics Student Version program* and all related software from your hard drive by completing the following steps:

⌨ *Click Start* → *Programs* → *Great Plains Dynamics Student Version* → *Uninstall Dynamics Student Version.*

⌨ *Click Yes in the Confirm File Deletion window when asked if you are sure you want to remove the selected application and all of its components.*

The uninstall process will take several seconds. When the process is done, you will receive a message saying that the process is complete. If there is also a message that some elements could not be removed, do the following:

⌨ *Click the OK button to close the Uninstall window.*

⌨ *Click Start* → *Programs* → *Windows Explorer.*

⌨ *Delete the Dynstdt folder and all of its contents from your hard drive.*

⌨ *Close Windows Explorer.*

You Use a Computer Laboratory or Other Computer Where you Will Most Likely Remove *Dynamics* Each Time you Stop Using the Computer

STEP 1. INSTALL THE *GREAT PLAINS DYNAMICS STUDENT VERSION* SOFTWARE. There are two methods for beginning the install process:

⌨ *With the computer on, insert the program CD into your CD-ROM drive. The setup window below should appear automatically in less than a minute.*

If this method does not automatically start the setup process, do the following:

⌨ *Make sure the program CD is in your CD-ROM drive. Click Start* → *Run. Type d:cdsetup.exe (where d: represents the drive letter of your CD-ROM drive). Click OK.* The setup window below will appear.

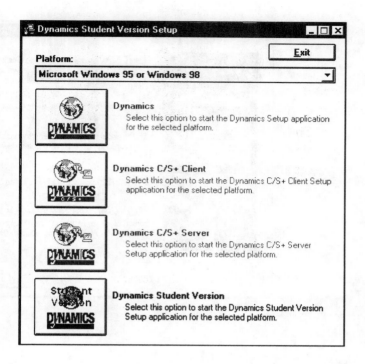

This is the first installation window. From this window you should:

- 💻 *Verify the Platform at the top of the window*. An example of a platform is Microsoft Windows 95 or 98. The installation program will detect the platform that you are using, but you can change the default if needed. It is unlikely that you will need to change it.
- 💻 *Click the Dynamics Student Version icon at the bottom of the window. If you are not ready to begin the installation, click Exit in the top right corner*.

Review the welcome and licensing information on the following screen:

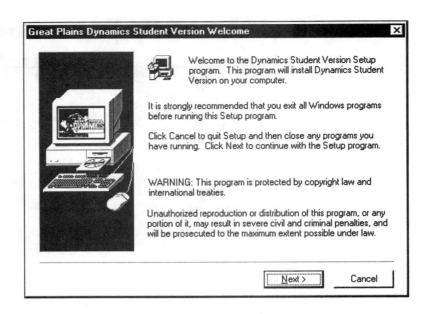

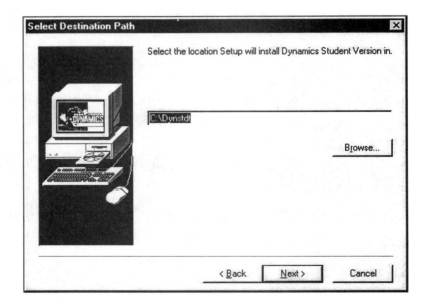

Click Next to continue. The following window appears:

Examine the directory that appears on this window to install the Dynamics Student Version. Click Next to continue.

If this directory has not been created, you will be prompted with a question window asking if you would like to create the directory. Click Yes to create the new directory if prompted. Otherwise, click Next.

The following window appears:

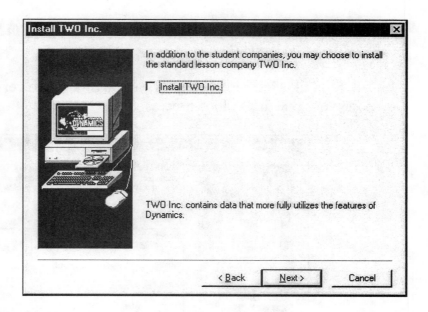

If you will be completing Chapter 5, which uses the sample company, The World Online (TWO Inc.), you should check the box to install TWO Inc. in the preceding window. This company takes an additional 30 megs of hard drive space to install.

Click the Install TWO Inc. box unless your instructor has informed you otherwise.

Click Next to continue.

The installation will include a *Great Plains Dynamics Student Version* option on your Start Program menu as shown on the following window.

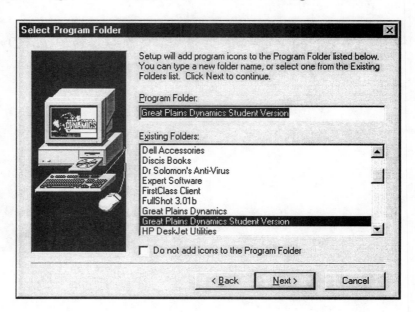

💻 *You need not make any changes in the settings in this window. Click Next to continue.*

The following window appears and allows you to verify the settings that you chose during the installation process.

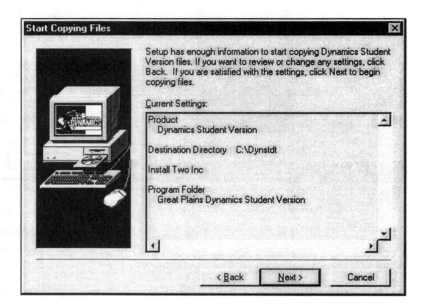

💻 *Click Next to continue.*

The setup software will begin copying *Great Plains Dynamics Student Version* files to the hard drive. Because there are a large number of files, installation may take several minutes.

You have completed installing the *Great Plains Dynamics Student Version* when the following window appears.

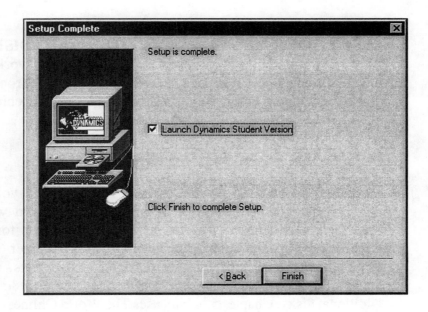

📇 *Assuming you plan to use the Great Plains Dynamics Student Version immediately, click Finish.* You will receive a Users and Companies Window like the one on page 2-3 (Chapter 2).

📇 *In the unlikely event that you would like to exit the program and use Dynamics at a later time, remove the check mark from the box in front of the words "Launch Dynamics Student Version" and then click Finish.*

After the installation is complete, go to Chapter 2 and begin to learn how to use *Dynamics* following those instructions, **but first read the following three paragraphs.**

You will need to install the software using the same procedures you have just completed in Step 1 each time you start using the *Great Plains Dynamics Student Version* software, assuming that you have uninstalled the software in Step 3.

You will follow Step 2 to back up your data files (pages 1-20 to 1-22) and Step 3 to uninstall the *Dynamics* software (pages 1-22 to 1-23) each time you stop using the computer in your laboratory. Refer back to that information then. Be sure you have two blank diskettes when you do so. When you finish Chapter 3, you should back up your data files following the procedures in Step 2, even if you plan to continue immediately to Chapter 4. Do the same at the end of Chapter 4, even if you plan to continue immediately to Chapter 5.

You will follow Step 4 (page 1-23) and Step 5 (pages 1-23 to 1-24) each time you start using the computer again, assuming that you uninstalled *Dynamics* when you stopped using the computer.

STEP 2. BACK UP YOUR DATA FILES ONTO DISKETTES. You should back up your data files to diskettes each time you stop working on the project. Do this because you will likely be uninstalling the software from the lab machine when you leave. Even if you leave the software on the lab machine, your data files may be corrupted by other lab users before you return.

Procedures to Back up Data Files

After completing a work session in *Dynamics*, you should back up the company data files to diskettes. For this project, you need two 3 1/2" diskettes: one for Waren Distributing (Chapter 4) data files and one for both Jackson Supply Company (Chapter 3) and Office Furniture Plus (Chapter 6) data files. Due to the large size of The World Online's (Chapter 5) data files, we do not recommend backing up this company's data files. If you decide to do so, you will need two additional disks. Chapter 5, which uses The World Online, can be completed in one sitting of 1-2 hours. We recommend that you complete Chapter 5 procedures in one sitting.

Before starting the backup process *for the first time*, it is recommended that you scan all diskettes to be used in the project. You do not need to scan the disks for subsequent backups. To scan a diskette, complete the following steps:

- ⌨ *Go to the MS-DOS prompt (Start → Programs → MS-DOS Prompt for most systems).*
- ⌨ *Type* [scandisk] *(don't include brackets) and press* [Return].
- ⌨ *When the ScanDisk window opens, select drive A.*
- ⌨ *Make sure the "Thorough" radio button is clicked and then click the Start button.*

If the disk scanning reveals no errors, use this disk for a backup disk. If there are errors, discard the disk and scan another one. Repeat the scanning procedures until you have all of the disks you need for the project.

- ⌨ *Exit all scanning-related windows.*

When you have the backup disks scanned, you are now ready to back up company data files.

⌨ *Exit the Dynamics program if it is open.*

⌨ *Click Start → Programs → Great Plains Dynamics Student Version →
Backup or Restore Dynamics Data.* The following window opens:

Dynamics Company Zip Window

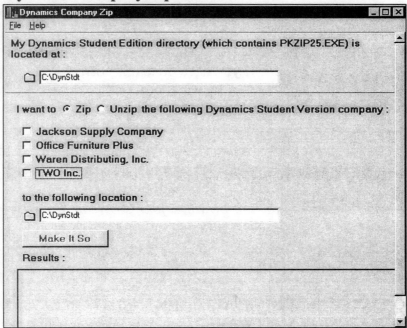

There are two radio buttons in this window: Zip (backup) and Unzip (restore).
Because the default is Zip, you do not have to do anything to these radio buttons
when backing up company data files.

The four companies used in this project are listed in the window and each
company has a blank check box next to it.

Recall that you should have two backup diskettes. One disk is used to back up
Waren Distributing, Inc. and one disk is used to back up both Jackson Supply
Company and Office Furniture Plus. A separate *.zip file will be created for each
company you back up. Because the default location for the backups is the Dynstdt
folder on the hard drive, you will have to change this to the A drive.

⌨ *Insert the appropriate diskette into the A drive.*

⌨ *Click the check box(es) to insert a check mark(s) **next to the company (companies) you want to back up. Be sure to select the correct company or companies.** Because Jackson Supply Company and Office Furniture Plus fit onto one disk, you can back up both companies simultaneously if you want to.*

⌨ *Click the yellow folder next to the "to the following location" box to open the Browse for Folder window. Select the A drive and click the OK button. If you have done this correctly, the following should appear in the "to the following location" box: A:\.*

⌨ *Click the "Make It So" box.*

The program will take several seconds to complete the backup process. When the process is done, the Results box will list what has been done.

⌨ *Repeat the previous four steps for the next company's (companies') backup(s).*

⌨ *When the last company backup is done, close the Dynamics Company Zip window.*

STEP 3. UNINSTALL THE *GREAT PLAINS DYNAMICS STUDENT VERSION* SOFTWARE. Each time you stop working on the project, you must uninstall the software if it is a requirement of the laboratory where you are doing the project.

CAUTION: This will remove all changes you have made to the company data, so you must back up your company data on diskettes before doing this if you want to continue working with the lesson.

Follow the instructions below to uninstall the software.

⌨ *Click Start → Programs → Great Plains Dynamics Student Version → Uninstall Dynamics Student Version.*

⌨ *Click Yes in the Confirm File Deletion window when asked if you are sure you want to remove the selected applications and all of its components.*

The uninstall process will take several seconds. When the Close the Uninstall window process is done, you will receive a message saying that the process is completed. If you get a message that "some elements could not be removed" instead of the "process is completed" message, do the following four steps.

- ▣ *Click the OK button to close the Uninstall window.*
- ▣ *Click Start → Programs → Windows Explorer.*
- ▣ *Delete the Dynstdt folder and all of its contents from the hard drive.*
- ▣ *Close Windows Explorer.*

STEP 4. REINSTALL THE *GREAT PLAINS DYNAMICS STUDENT VERSION* SOFTWARE. Assuming you have uninstalled the software in Step 3, you must reinstall the software again the next time you work on the project. This step is the same as Step 1 (pages 1-14 to 1-19), so follow those instructions.

STEP 5. RESTORE YOUR DATA FILES FROM EXTERNAL DISKETTES. You will need to restore your data files each time you reinstall the *Dynamics* software. Also, you may want to restore certain data files if you decide to redo a portion of the project.

Procedures to Restore Data Files

The *Dynamics* Company Zip window is also used to restore company data files from the backup diskettes to the company data files in the *Dynamics* application program. To restore company data files, complete the following steps:

- ▣ *Exit the Dynamics program if it is open.*
- ▣ *Click Start → Programs → Great Plains Dynamics Student Version → Backup or Restore Dynamics Data to open the Dynamics Company Zip window.*
- ▣ *Click the Unzip (restore) radio button.*
- ▣ *Insert the appropriate backup diskette into the A drive. **Be sure to insert the correct backup diskette for the company (companies) you are restoring.***
- ▣ *Click the check box(es) to insert a check mark(s) next to the company (companies) you are restoring. **Be sure to select the correct company or companies**. If you had backed up Jackson Supply Company and Office Furniture Plus on the same diskette, you can restore them simultaneously from that backup diskette.*

    ⌨ *Check the "from the following location" box to make sure that the A drive [A:\] is selected. If not, click the yellow folder next to the box to open the Browse for Folder window. Select the A drive and click the OK button.* If you have done this correctly, the following should appear in the "from the following location" box: A:\.

    ⌨ *Click the "Make It So" button.*

The program will take several seconds to complete the restore process. When the process is done, the Results box will list what has been done.

    ⌨ *Repeat the previous three steps for the next company or companies whose data set(s) you want to restore.*

    ⌨ *When the last company data set is restored, close the Dynamics Company Zip window.*

If you decide that you want to do an entire chapter over again because you have made errors or want additional practice, you should do the following three steps:

1.   Back up your data files on diskettes for all chapters that you DO NOT want to redo (see Step 2 on pages 1-20 to 1-22).

2.   Install the *Great Plains Dynamics Student Version* software (see Step 1 on pages 1-14 to 1-19). Doing so will replace all company data files with the original data files from the installation CD.

3.   Use your backup diskettes to restore *only the data files for the chapters you DO NOT want to do again*. For example, if you decide to redo Chapter 4, but are satisfied with Chapters 2 and 3, you should restore Jackson Supply Company and Office Furniture Plus, but not Waren Distributing Inc. You will be doing Waren Distributing over again in Chapter 4.

CHAPTER 2

Familiarization

This chapter illustrates features of *Dynamics* and provides practice using the program so that you will be able to complete assignments for the project. **Do not skip this chapter**.

The discussion assumes that you have a working knowledge of Windows 98 or Windows 95. If you need additional guidance for using Windows, consult your Windows user manual.

Entering the *Dynamics* Program and a Company

Starting now, you will be using the computer to perform tasks on *Dynamics*. In this chapter, the instructions are reasonably detailed to make certain that you understand how to use *Dynamics* correctly and efficiently.

The Instructions and Assignments book and the Reference book provide instructions and display window illustrations in a Windows 95 format. If you are using Windows 98, certain window functions and the appearance of the windows will differ slightly. However, the *Dynamics* elements and functions are identical between Windows 95 and Windows 98.

Do not be concerned about making mistakes while performing familiarization activities in this chapter. It is important that you practice each activity and learn by doing.

If, at any time, you decide that you want to start the chapter again, you may do so by installing *Dynamics* software again following Step 1 of the installation instructions in Chapter 1. You may want to do so if you believe that you do not understand the material in the chapter. If you install the *Dynamics* software again, all previous *Dynamics* software and related data files are overwritten.

To begin using *Dynamics*, complete the following step. If you have just completed loading the *Dynamics* software, the window on the following page should be on your screen. If so, go to the next page. You will follow the instructions below when you start the project in the future.

- To start the program:

   💻 *Click Start → Programs → Great Plains Dynamics Student Version → Great Plains Dynamics*. (The → means that you do the steps sequentially. For the previous steps, first click Start. After the Start menu appears, click Programs. After the Programs menu appears, click *Great Plains Dynamics Student Version*, and so on until you enter *Dynamics*.)

The window shown below appears.

Users and Companies Window

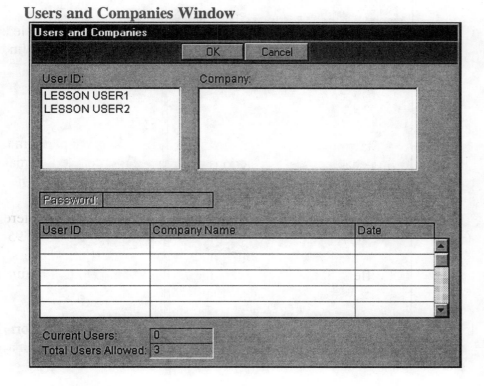

This window is used to select your User ID and to select the company you want to work with. After the User ID and the company are selected, the *Dynamics* main window appears. Your User ID is LESSON USER1.

Click once on LESSON USER1 and observe that a list of companies appears in the Company box. Next, click once on the sample company, Jackson Supply Company and click the OK button at the top of the window.

After Jackson Supply Company is opened, the following *Dynamics* main window appears:

Dynamics Main Window

NOTE: There is more than one way to complete many activities in *Dynamics*. For example, an alternative way to open a company is to double-click on the company name. To keep the instructions as simple as practical in the project, only one method of doing an activity is normally provided.

Observe that the top right portion of the window provides your User ID [LESSON USER1], the name of the company you are working on [Jackson Supply Company], and the current date. This information lets you know that you accessed the correct company.

This window is important in using *Dynamics* because it is the starting point for all other activities. The *Dynamics* main window also appears in the background whenever you access additional *Dynamics* windows. You must feel comfortable entering and exiting the window.

⌨ *Click ⊠ in the top right corner to exit the program or click the File menu and then click Exit.*

⌨ *Follow the instructions on pages 2-2 and 2-3 to open the Dynamics program and Jackson Supply Company again.*

⌨ *Repeat these two steps until you feel comfortable that you can exit and enter the Dynamics main window and access a company on the list.*

The Menu Bar

The menu bar at the top of the *Dynamics* main window is used to select setup options and system-wide commands in *Dynamics*. See the top of the window on page 2-4 for the menu bar. The menu bar is also shown below. It is similar to the menu bar in most Windows applications, but other than the Help menu, it is not used extensively in the project. Because of the similarities to other Windows applications and its infrequent use, it is not discussed further here. See pages 2-25 to 2-27 for a discussion of the *Dynamics* Help menu if you ever need additional assistance.

Menu Bar

File	Edit	Tools	Setup	Utilities	Windows	Help

Using the Tool Bar and Palettes

Every activity in *Dynamics* involves using one or more windows. An example of a *Dynamics* window is shown on page 2-13. There are dozens of windows in *Dynamics*, with each permitting an efficient and effective way to complete activities.

You will use the tool bar and palettes to access windows. The tool bar categorizes accounting tasks by function such as transaction recording, maintenance, and report preparation. A specific tool bar button is used to select a palette. There are several palettes for each tool bar button. Each palette categorizes windows by accounting activities. For example, in the Sales Transactions palette, the accounting activities include invoice entry, cash receipts, and several others. The user selects an accounting activity on a palette to select a specific window. The combination of tool bar buttons and palette window options permits the convenient selection of many different accounting activity windows.

The tool bar is the row of six buttons on the second line of the *Dynamics* main window. You will be using several of these in this chapter. See page 2-4 for their location on the main window. The tool bar buttons are also shown below and the use of each button is explained.

Tool Bar

- **Transactions** — Used to open windows in which transactions are processed. Most of the work performed in the project is done through the Transactions button.

- **Inquiry** — Used to review information in the system for recorded transactions and other records.

- **Reports** — Provides access to options used to print reports and simplify the printing process.

- **Cards** — Used to create and maintain master file information, such as customer and vendor records.

- **Routines** — Used to set up groups of tasks to be performed in a certain order within a certain time frame. An example of a task that is performed through the Routines button is the periodic aging of accounts receivable.

- **Work** — Used to quickly access *Dynamics* palettes and windows that are used frequently. The Work button is a more advanced feature and is not used in the project.

Observe that the first four tool bar buttons (Transactions, Inquiry, Reports, and Cards) closely parallel the last four key activities in the project discussed in Chapter 1 on page 1-5.

As discussed previously, there are many different palettes within *Dynamics*. An illustration of a typical palette, the Purchasing Trx (Transactions) palette, is shown next. To access this palette from the *Dynamics* main window:

🖳 *Click Transactions → Purchasing.*

Typical Palette

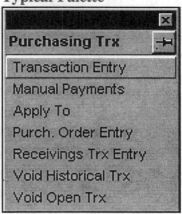

 Close the Purchasing Trx palette by clicking the ☒ *in the top right corner of the palette.* Caution: Be careful not to click the ☒ in the top right corner of the *Dynamics* main window because this will close the entire *Dynamics* program and send you back to your computer's start-up screen.

The flow of commands used to reach a desired window is always as follows, in the order listed:

1. Click once on the desired tool bar button to show that button's palette options.
2. Click once on the desired palette option to show the list of available window options within the chosen palette.
3. Click once on the desired window option to select the desired activity window.

To avoid repeating these commands each time you are asked to select a window, a short command is used in the project. For example, to open the Payables Transaction Entry window in the project, the following command flow is given [don't enter this now, however]:

> *Transactions* → *Purchasing* → *Transaction Entry*
> [Tool bar button]   [Palette option]   [Window option]

Don't be concerned about getting into the wrong window. It is easy to get out of a window by pressing ☒ in the top right corner of the window. These materials will provide guidance to get you into the appropriate window for each task in the project.

Practice Selecting Windows Using the Tool Bar and Palettes

To practice accessing *Dynamics* windows using the tool bar and palettes, complete the following steps:

- *Click Transactions → Sales → Cash Receipts to access the Cash Receipts Entry window.* This window is used to enter a cash receipt. The top of the window should read Cash Receipts Entry.

- *Close the Cash Receipts Entry window to return to the Dynamics main window. Close the window by clicking the ⊠ in the top right corner of the Cash Receipts Entry window.* Again, be careful not to click the ⊠ in the top right corner of the entire computer screen. Remember that this will close the *Dynamics* program and send you back to your computer's start-up screen.

- *Click Cards → Inventory → Item to access the Item Maintenance window.* This window is used to add, delete, or modify an inventory item. Do not close this window yet.

- *Click Reports → Financial → Financial Statements to access the Financial Statement Report window.* This window is used to print financial statements to the screen or to a printer. Notice that the Item Maintenance window is still open behind the Financial Statement Report window. It is acceptable to have more than one window open or to close a window when you are not using it.

- *Close the Financial Statement Report window.* Notice that the Item Maintenance window is still open.

- *Close the Item Maintenance window to return to the Dynamics main window.*

The Reference book contains several sections with instructions for recording transactions and performing maintenance and other tasks using *Dynamics* windows. In order to limit repetition in the project, the Reference book materials *do not* instruct you to close each window when you have finished recording a transaction or completing a maintenance or other task. When you are done with each window, either use the window again to record another transaction or complete another task, or close the window.

A Typical *Dynamics* Window

In this section, you will explore a typical *Dynamics* window and practice using some common features of *Dynamics* windows.

🖥 *Click Transactions* ➜ *Sales* ➜ *Invoice Entry.*

The Invoice Entry window appears on the screen. The window should look like the one on page 2-13, except it will not include the circled letters. This window is an example of a typical window for recording transactions in *Dynamics*. You will be using this type of window extensively in later assignments.

If the entire window is not visible on your screen, it will be extremely helpful to make it so by hiding the Windows taskbar at the bottom of your screen. You can hide the Windows taskbar by completing the following steps:

🖥 *Close the Invoice Entry window.*
🖥 *Click Start* ➜ *Settings* ➜ *Taskbar to open the Taskbar Properties window.*
🖥 *Click the Auto hide check box so that a check mark appears in the box.*
🖥 *Click the OK button to close the Taskbar Properties window.*
🖥 *Click Transactions* ➜ *Sales* ➜ *Invoice Entry to reopen the Invoice Entry window.*

The Windows taskbar will now appear *only* when you move the mouse pointer to the bottom of the screen. When the mouse pointer is anywhere else on the screen, the taskbar is hidden and all *Dynamics* windows will fit on the screen. To cancel the Auto hide function, repeat the previous steps and remove the check mark in the Auto hide box.

🖥 *Move the mouse pointer to the bottom of the screen to observe that the taskbar reopens.*

Next, you will use the Invoice Entry window to practice using common *Dynamics* features. The window includes many **description fields**, **entry boxes** that are completed with **default information**, empty **entry boxes**, and various symbols. These will be explained in the next few pages and you will practice using them.

- **Description fields.** These fields include labels which describe the information that must be typed, selected, or accepted to complete the window. For example, Document Type, Document No., Hold, and Date are all description fields in the Invoice Entry window on your screen and on page 2-13. Each description field corresponds to an entry box where information is to be entered.

- **Entry boxes.** Entry boxes are typically directly below the description fields, but are sometimes also located to the right or elsewhere. For example, the word "Invoice" is included in the entry box directly below the description field "Document Type", whereas the entry box under Batch ID is blank. At the bottom left of the window, there are blank entry boxes to the right of Trade Discount, Freight and so on. For simplicity, the term "box" will be used throughout the remainder of the project, instead of "entry box".

- **Default information.** Observe that the Document Type box now includes "Invoice." Invoice is the **default setting** for the Document Type box, which means that you can accept Invoice in that box without entering any information. Default settings are established through maintenance to reduce the time needed to enter information. Default settings are one of the most important benefits of computerized accounting software.

Moving Through Boxes

The Return (Enter) key on your keyboard is used extensively in *Dynamics*. The Return key is used to move to the next box in a window. It is used to skip through boxes that you want to leave blank, to accept default data, or to move to the next box after you have entered data. Note: You may also use the Tab key to move through boxes, but the project materials assume you are using the Return key.

To move the cursor backward through the boxes that already include information or ones that have been skipped, hold the Shift key down while pressing the Tab key. You can also use the mouse to move the cursor to a previous box.

For now, you are only learning to use the Return key and Shift/Tab keys without concern for the contents of the boxes.

⌨ *Press [Return] three or four times and watch the cursor on the screen as it moves repeatedly from one box to another.* Note that when you move into certain boxes, default information appears (for example, in the Document No. box).

⌨ *Next, hold the Shift key down and press [Tab] enough times to move the cursor back to the Document Type box.*

⌨ *Press [Return] repeatedly, attempting to move the cursor into the Item Number box.* Note that after moving out of the Customer PO Number box, you receive an error message that says, "Please enter a customer ID," which indicates you did not complete certain necessary information.

⌨ *Click the OK button to remove the error message.* Your cursor should be in the Batch ID box, one box before the Customer ID box.

Observe that the Customer ID description field, as well as other description fields in the window, are shown in bold black print. This indicates that these are required boxes and you must enter data in them before completing the window, and in some cases, before moving beyond them. Observe that in addition to Customer ID, Document Type, Document No., Date, and Name are all required boxes.

⌨ *Now enter the Customer ID box by clicking once on that box. Note: Do not click the description field "Customer ID", but click the empty box below the description field. Practice using the mouse to enter different boxes until you feel comfortable.*

To summarize, note that you can move successfully through a window by pressing the Return key (Shift/Tab keys for reverse movement) or you can enter boxes not in succession by using the mouse.

You should not use the Shift/Return keys on the keyboard to move backward through boxes. To show why, do the following:

⌨ *Return to the Invoice Entry window if you are not already there. With the cursor in any one of the boxes, hold the Shift key down and press the Return key.* You should get an error window which says, "Unable to save. The transaction is not assigned to a batch." Attempting to use Shift/Return to move backward in a window causes *Dynamics* to attempt to save the entire transaction, rather than the contents of the box.

⌨ *Click the OK button to remove the error message and return to the Invoice Entry window.*

⌨ *Close the Invoice Entry window that you've been practicing in by clicking the ⊠ in the top right corner of the transaction window.* [Remember: not the top right corner of the computer screen.] *If you get a window asking if you want to save or delete this record, click the Delete button.*

⌨ *Return to the Invoice Entry window by clicking Transactions ➔ Sales ➔ Invoice Entry.* Observe that you now have an empty Invoice Entry window.

In most *Dynamics* windows used in this project, there are boxes in which you do not need to enter information. Either the default information is correct or the information is not applicable to the transactions. The Reference book instructions for recording each type of transaction in *Dynamics* focus on boxes in which you need to perform some type of activity, such as typing information or selecting an option from a list of available choices. *If a box is not discussed, you do not have to do anything with that box.* For example, if the document number box is not mentioned in the instructions for a specific *Dynamics* window, the default entry is correct and you can therefore press the Return key to go to the next box.

Next, the inclusion of default information in boxes is discussed. Observe that the Document Type box now includes the word "Invoice" and the Document No. box is blank.

⌨ *Press the Return key and observe that a document number — 5128 — appears in the Document No. box.*

You have moved to a second box and, by doing so, you have accepted Invoice as the default setting for the Document Type box.

💻 *Press [Return] again and observe that you are now in the Hold box and have thereby accepted the default Document No. as 5128 (invoice #5128).*

💻 *Press [Return] again and observe that you are in the Date box.*

💻 *Press [Return] again and observe that you are in the Default Site box, which says MAIN, and have thereby accepted the default setting for the date. Press [Return] again to move into the first blank box without a default setting, Batch ID.*

Later, there is a discussion and illustration of changing a box that includes default information.

Entering Information Into Boxes

There are different ways to enter information into the boxes of a window or show that information. The circled letters A through I in the diagram of the Invoice Entry window shown below correspond with the discussion in the following nine sections: drop-down list boxes, lookup buttons, date boxes, check boxes, text boxes, show and hide buttons, expansion buttons, zoom feature, and additional window buttons. Finally, the redisplay function is explained even though it cannot be illustrated in the Invoice Entry window below.

A Typical *Dynamics* Window — Invoice Entry

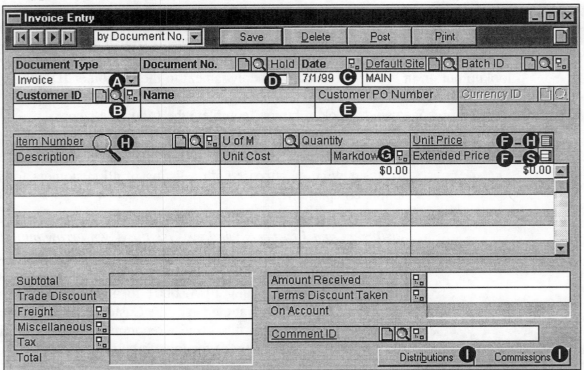

A. Drop-down List Boxes

Drop-down list boxes are identifiable by an adjacent down arrow button, as shown above. Clicking the arrow button allows you to see a list of available choices. To select an item from a drop-down list, click once on the item.

An example of a drop-down list in the Invoice Entry is the first box in the window, the Document Type box. To practice using the Document Type drop-down list, complete the following steps:

- *Click once on the Document Type drop-down list arrow button.* A list of the two available document types drops below the box: Invoice or Return.

- *Click once on Return and then press the Return key to accept the selection and move to the next box.* Observe that the default Document No. changes to match the next sequential return document number, 1502.

- *Click the Document Type drop-down arrow again and select Invoice as the option.* Observe again the Document No. changes back to the next default invoice number, 5128.

B. Lookup Buttons

Lookup buttons are identifiable by a magnifying glass symbol . They are an extremely handy and often used feature in *Dynamics*. Clicking a lookup button allows you to see a list of available choices for the adjacent box. An example of a lookup button in the Invoice Entry window is next to the Customer ID box.

To practice using a lookup button, complete the following steps:

- *Click once on the Customer ID lookup button.* The Customers and Prospects window appears with a listing of all customers for the sample company.

- *Locate the up/down scrolling arrows on the right side of the Customers and Prospects window. Use the down arrow button to locate The Plaza Suites, Customer ID PLAZ0001, and double-click on its line.* Note: The same information can be entered by clicking once on the line containing PLAZ0001 to highlight it and then clicking the Select button at the top of the Customers and Prospects window. For simplicity, this project recommends using the first method (double-click method) for lookup buttons.

Assume that the goods sold to The Plaza Suites will be shipped from a different location than that listed in the Default Site box (MAIN).

🖥 *Click the Default Site lookup button* (next to the Default Site description field). The MAIN site is highlighted because it is the default entry.

🖥 *Click the up arrow on the right side of the Item Sites scrolling window to show the other location, EAST. Double click EAST and the Default Site box will now show EAST.*

Next, assume you realize that Jackson Supply Company doesn't ship anything out of its EAST site because there is no inventory there.

🖥 *Click the Default Site lookup button again and select the MAIN warehouse location.*

For additional practice using lookup buttons, use the lookup button for Item Number to bill the customer for one set of draperies, item #112.

🖥 *Click the Item Number lookup button, find item #112 and double-click the line.* Note that you need to scroll down the list of inventory items using the down arrow button to find item #112.

C. Date Boxes

Most *Dynamics* windows include Date boxes for entering the date of transactions. In most cases, the default entry in the date box will be the current date, which appears in the top right corner of the *Dynamics* main window. To accept the default date when entering a transaction, press [Return] when the cursor is in the Date box. To change the date, move to the Date box, make sure the entire date is highlighted (you may have to use the mouse to highlight the date), and type the date using 2 digits each for the month, day of the month, and the last two digits of the year. For example, assume that the date of the sale to The Plaza Suites was February 7, 1998.

🖥 *Use the mouse to highlight the entire default date in the Date box.*
🖥 *Type [020798] and press [Return].*

D. Check Boxes ☑

A check box represents an option that is chosen when the box is checked. To "check" such a box or to remove an existing check mark, click once on the box. For example, in the Invoice Entry window, the Hold box is a check box. The Hold box allows the user to complete the transaction, but not post it so that it can be edited later. To practice using the check box, complete the following:

> 💻 *Click once on the Hold check box. Observe that a check mark is placed there.*
>
> 💻 *Remove the check by clicking the check box again. Be sure the box is unchecked before continuing.*

E. Text Boxes

Text boxes are boxes in which you type data. An example of a text box in the Invoice Entry window is the Customer PO Number box. The Plaza Suites issued purchase order #RQ68295 for the sale.

> 💻 *Click the Customer PO Number box to enter the box.*
>
> 💻 *Type [RQ68295] in the Customer PO Number box and press [Return].* The purchase order number should appear in the Customer PO Number text box.

Assume that the correct purchase order number is #QR86529. The next step illustrates the *incorrect* way to edit existing information in a text box.

> 💻 *Click the Customer PO box so that the cursor appears to the left of the "R" in the purchase order number.*
>
> 💻 *Try to type the new purchase order number.*

Notice that the old purchase order number remains to the right of the information you typed. This is because *Dynamics* requires you to either delete the old information or highlight all of the old information with the mouse before typing new information.

> 💻 *Delete all information in the Customer PO box.*
>
> 💻 *Type the correct purchase order number and press [Return].*

To illustrate the highlight method of editing information in a text box, do the following:

> ⌨ *Use the mouse to highlight **all** of the new purchase order number.*
>
> ⌨ *Type the old purchase order number again (RQ68295) and press [Return].*

F. Show and Hide Buttons (F-S = Show ▣   F-H = Hide ▣)

An example of a description field and box configuration is in the middle of the Invoice Entry window where there are two rows of description fields followed by several blank rows of boxes. The first row of description fields includes: Item Number, U of M, Quantity, and Unit Price. The second row of description fields includes: Description, Unit Cost, Markdown, and Extended Price. The blank boxes in the scrolling window beneath the two rows of description fields are used to enter information for each inventory item sold.

First, you will use the Show and Hide buttons to change the appearance of the boxes. Observe that the information you already entered for item #112 is in the first row of boxes.

> ⌨ *Click the Show button (**F-S** in the diagram on page 2-13, ▣). Notice that another row of information is added for item #112. Immediately below the two lines of information for item #112 are two blank lines in a different shade, then two blank lines in the same shade. Each set of two lines is for the sale of a different product on the same invoice.*

To hide the additional lines of information once the Show button has been clicked, click the Hide button. The Hide button is immediately above the Show button (**F-H** in the diagram on page 2-13, ▣).

> ⌨ *Click the Hide button. Now there are five blank lines below item #112. Each line is for the sale of another product on the same invoice.*
>
> ⌨ *Click the Show button again to leave two lines of information displayed for each inventory item sold.*

It is important to understand which information is in each box. The descriptions fields are in the two rows above the blank boxes in the scrolling window. Because there are two rows of boxes for each product being sold, there are also two rows of description fields.

The letters on the scrolling window illustration below correspond to the description fields at the top of the scrolling window. The letters a through h correspond to the information requested and calculated in the entry boxes, as follows:

a. Item Number   e. Description
b. U of M (unit of measure)   f. Unit Cost
c. Quantity   g. Markdown
d. Unit Price   h. Extended Price

The first two rows of invoice data, indicated by the subscript 1, contain all of the information about the first inventory item sold on this invoice. The next two rows (subscript 2) are for the second inventory item sold. The next two rows (subscript 3) are for the third inventory item sold, etc.

Item Number		U of M	Quantity		Unit Price	
Description		Unit Cost		Markdown	Extended Price	
a_1		b_1	c_1		d_1	
e_1		f_1		g_1	h_1	
a_2		b_2	c_2		d_2	
e_2		f_2		g_2	h_2	
a_3		b_3	c_3		d_3	
e_3		f_3		g_3	h_3	

▪ *Click the Hide button. Notice that only the boxes for Item Number, U of M, Quantity, and Unit Price are shown, whereas the four boxes in the second row are hidden.*

▪ *Click the blank Item Number box below "112" or press the Return key until the cursor reaches this box.*

▪ *Use the Lookup button and select item #105.*

▪ *Type [25] in the Quantity box for the number of units being sold.*

▪ *Press [Return] until the cursor reaches the blank Item Number box below "105".*

▪ *Complete row three by selecting item #108, with 10 units sold.*

▪ *Press [Return] until the cursor reaches the blank Item Number box below "108".*

▪ *Complete row four by selecting product 109, with 20 units invoiced.*

▪ *Press [Return] until the cursor reaches the blank Item Number box below "109". The total on the bottom of the window should now be $2,195.82.*

⌨ *Click the Show button and observe that all eight boxes of information are now shown for each product. Use the scroll button on the right of the window to view all four products.*

⌨ *Click the Delete button at the top of the window to indicate that you do not want to post the transaction, then click Delete again when asked whether you want to delete the record.*

Now, enter all of the previous information in the Invoice Entry Window for Plaza Suites, only this time with the two rows of information showing for each product.

⌨ *Use the Customer ID lookup button to select Plaza Suites.*

⌨ *Type [RQ68295] in the Customer PO Box.*

⌨ *Select the product number for each of the four products and type the quantity sold in the Quantity box. Press Return to scroll through the remaining boxes for each item until the cursor reaches the next blank Item Number box. After entering all information and moving the cursor to the blank Item Number box below "Standard comforter", the total at the bottom of the window should be $2,195.82.*

⌨ *Click the Hide button to show only the top row of each product.*

You can enter information in boxes in scrolling windows with all rows shown or with certain rows hidden. Most people prefer to enter the information with most rows hidden because it requires less moving through boxes. It is usually desirable to then use the Show button to look at all information for accuracy.

G. Expansion Buttons

An expansion button is used to open a window where information for the box next to the expansion button can be added, changed, or viewed. In the Invoice Entry window, an expansion button appears to the right of the Markdown description field. The Plaza Suites will receive a ten percent markdown on the 10 blankets sold (item #108). To practice using the expansion button, complete the following steps:

> *Click the Show button to reveal two rows of boxes for each item sold.*

> *Make sure the cursor is in one of the boxes for item #108, the blankets. It does not matter which box it is in (Item Number, Quantity, U of M, etc.), but Dynamics needs to know that you're entering information for the blankets, not for any other item. Click the Markdown expansion button.* The Invoice Markdown Entry window appears.

> *Change the markdown from zero to ten percent (10.00%) and click the OK button to return to the Invoice Entry window.* Notice that a ten percent markdown, $2.35 per unit, appears in the Markdown box for item #108.

H. Zoom Feature

While working in *Dynamics*, you will notice that sometimes the mouse pointer turns into a magnifying glass when it passes over certain description fields within a window. The magnifying glass is larger than the one used for lookup buttons. The magnifying glass indicates that additional information is available for those fields. When you click the magnifying glass on such a field, the program "zooms" to a window containing additional information. Zoom fields are shown in an underlined font in all windows.

When a zoom field contains an account balance, you can go all the way back to an originating transaction window. Zoom fields containing other information are used to access master file records, such as customer and vendor records.

There are five zoom fields in the Invoice Entry window: Default Site, Customer ID, Item Number, Unit Price, and Comment ID. Note that all five of these zoom fields are shown in an underlined font. Complete the following steps to practice the zoom feature:

> *Move the mouse pointer over the Customer ID description field. Note that the cursor must be directly over the words "Customer ID", not in the Customer ID entry box. When the mouse pointer turns into a magnifying glass, click once.*

The Customer Maintenance window for The Plaza Suites appears on the screen. This window contains the customer record for The Plaza Suites and is used to view, add, delete, or change default information for the customer.

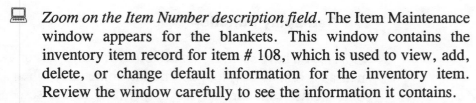

> 💻 *Close the Customer Maintenance window to return to the Invoice Entry window.*
>
> 💻 *Make sure the cursor is still in one of the boxes for item #108, the blankets. Move the mouse pointer over the Unit Price description field (the description field over the scrolling window, not the Unit Price box for the blankets) until the pointer turns into a magnifying glass and click once.*

The Item Pricing Inquiry window appears for item #108. Notice that there is another zoom field in this window: the Item Number description field in the top left corner of the window.

> 💻 *Zoom on the Item Number description field.* The Item Maintenance window appears for the blankets. This window contains the inventory item record for item # 108, which is used to view, add, delete, or change default information for the inventory item. Review the window carefully to see the information it contains.
>
> 💻 *Close the Item Maintenance window and then close the Item Pricing Inquiry window to return to the Invoice Entry window.*

I. Additional Window Buttons

To record a transaction in *Dynamics*, often you must enter information into two or more windows. When more than one window is needed to record a transaction, *Dynamics* makes it easy to access the additional window(s) by using buttons in the bottom right corner of the main transaction entry window.

In the Invoice Entry window, there are two additional window buttons in the bottom right corner: Distributions and Commissions. You will practice using the Distributions button because it appears in many *Dynamics* windows and is necessary to enter general ledger posting information for most transactions.

> 💻 *Click the Distributions button.* The Invoice Distribution Entry window appears. *Dynamics* has already distributed the sales transaction to various general ledger accounts using information it has on file for the selected customer and inventory items sold.
>
> 💻 *Click the Show button (above right side of scrolling window) to view the account name for each general ledger account.*

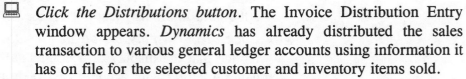

The default posting account for the markdown is account #30100, Sales, but assume the markdown for this transaction should be posted to account #30300, Sales Discounts. Complete the following steps to correct the posting account:

⌨ *Move the cursor anywhere within the five digits of account #30100 on the line containing the markdown portion of the transaction ($23.50).*

⌨ *Click the lookup button adjacent to the Account description field above the scrolling window. Note: do not **zoom** on the Account description field, but click the Account lookup button.*

⌨ *Select account #30300, Sales Discounts, as the posting account for the markdown.*

⌨ *Click the OK button to save the general ledger account information and return to the Invoice Entry window. Do not exit the Invoice Entry window yet.*

J.   Redisplay Function

As you have seen, *Dynamics* often displays lists of available choices for a box, such as a box with a lookup button. Sometimes when *Dynamics* displays a list, some items from the list are not visible on the screen because of screen size limitations. The redisplay option repositions cursor control to the beginning of the list. To illustrate an example of this feature:

⌨ *Click the Distributions button again in the lower right corner of the Invoice Entry window for the Plaza Suites invoice.* The Invoice Distribution Entry window will come up with the account number for Taxes, #20800 highlighted.

Assume that you want to scan the general ledger list to check that the proper account for taxes has been used. Do the following:

⌨ *With the account number 20800 highlighted, click on the lookup button next to the Account description field.* A list of the general ledger accounts appears, beginning with the highlighted account number, #20800. All general ledger account numbers prior to 20800 are in the list, just not visible.

⌨ *Click the Redisplay button at the top of the Accounts window.* Notice that the display of accounts shifts to the beginning of the general ledger with account #10100 for Cash—General Account. You can also use the up arrow to scroll to the beginning of the list, but Redisplay does it quicker.

⌨ *Close the Accounts window and the Invoice Distribution Entry window.* Do not close the Invoice Entry window.

Correcting a Transaction Before Posting

Before a transaction is posted, most errors can be corrected by clicking the box with the error and making the correction. For many errors, you can click the box with the error and reenter the correct information.

For other boxes, error correction is a bit more complicated. An example of one of these boxes is the Item Number box. Assume that the last item sold to The Plaza Suites should have been item #107, a set of two pillows, instead of item #109, the comforters.

> 💻 *Click the Item Number box for the last item, item #109. Use the scroll button to locate item #109 if necessary. Note: Be sure to click the Item Number box, not the Item Number description field.*

> 💻 *Click the Item Number lookup button and attempt to select item #107.*

An error message appears saying that you cannot change items. To correct the error, do the following:

> 💻 *Click OK to remove the error message.*

> 💻 *Make sure the cursor is somewhere in any box for item #109. Click the Edit menu at the very top of the screen, and click the Delete Row option. A message appears asking you if you are sure that you want to delete this item. Click the Delete button.*

> 💻 *Press [Return] to move through the boxes for the third item, item #108, until the cursor is in the Item Number box for the next item to be sold.*

> 💻 *Enter the sale of item #107, 1 set of pillows.*

Certain boxes cannot be changed after they are originally completed. Changes in these boxes can only be made by deleting the transaction and entering the transaction again, which is described in the next section.

Deleting a Transaction Before Posting

After a transaction is posted in *Dynamics*, it cannot be changed or deleted. This is so important that it is worth repeating **often**. You should make every effort to be sure a transaction is correct before it is posted.

You can delete a transaction *prior* to posting by clicking the Delete button at the top of the transaction window. Deleting a transaction before posting is useful if there is an error on the window that cannot be corrected. An example in the Invoice Entry window is the Customer ID box. For example, assume you discover that you selected the wrong customer for the practice sale. The sale was made to The Columbus Inn, customer ID # COLU0001, not The Plaza Suites.

> ⌨ *Try to click the Customer ID lookup button. Dynamics* will not let you change the customer ID. You must delete the transaction and start over again.

> ⌨ *Click the Delete button at the top of the Invoice Entry window. Dynamics* asks you if you are sure you want to delete this record.

> ⌨ *Click Delete to answer the question.* Notice that the Invoice Entry window is now blank. Do not close the Invoice Entry window yet.

Correcting a Transaction After Posting

In using *Dynamics*, it is important to avoid posting a transaction that is in error. After a transaction is posted, you cannot edit or delete the transaction. Depending on the type of transaction, you must first either void the transaction or record a transaction that removes the effects of the transaction in error. Next, you must record another transaction with the correct information. In some cases, error correction is quite difficult.

Four strategies are suggested to minimize the likelihood of errors after posting.

- **Starting in Chapter 3, follow the guidance in the Reference book for each transaction.** Completing a window may appear simple after you have practiced a couple of times, but it is easy to make mistakes.

- **Enter all information carefully.** There is often a penalty for excessive speed.

- **Read the instructions and hints very carefully as you proceed.** The materials have been class tested several times and hints are provided where you are most likely to make mistakes.

- **Review each window carefully before posting or saving.** It is worth the time it takes to review each *Dynamics* window. Frequently, check figures are provided to help you minimize errors.

Specific instructions for error correction are included in Appendix A of the Reference book. Because Chapter 3 is for practice, error correction applies primarily to Chapters 4, 5 and 6. You may, however, practice using Appendix A to correct errors you make in Chapter 3.

An option that you may find easier, especially for errors that are very difficult to correct, is to start the chapter over by reinstalling the *Dynamics* software. An even better option is to avoid posting transactions that are in error by following the preceding four strategies.

Dynamics Help Menu

Now that you have reviewed the features of a typical *Dynamics* window, you will explore the Help menu. Like many Windows-based programs, *Dynamics* has extensive online documentation available for your reference. There are many selections in the Help menu, but the two most common features that you will use are:

- **Index** — Displays an alphabetical list of all help topics. When you enter the Help index, type in a key word for a specific topic that you want to learn more about.

- **About This Item** — Displays online documentation for an active window or box. To display the online documentation for a specific box, click the box, then click "About This Item" from the Help menu.

Dynamics Help Menu — Practice

To practice using the Help index, complete the following steps while still in the Invoice Entry window:

⌨ *Click the Help menu and then click Index.* Suppose that you want to know how to record a sales return.

⌨ *Type [returns].* Notice that the portion of the Help index now displayed contains several topics under the heading: "returns."

⌨ *Double-click the line that says "entering sales returns."* A Help window appears on the screen describing how to record invoices and sales returns in *Dynamics*. Notice the many links (underlined and in a different color) that the Help material provides to other useful information.

⌨ *Close the Help window.*

Next, assume you are working with the Invoice Entry window and want to know what the Trade Discount box is used for and how to enter information in the box. Complete the following steps to practice the "About This Item" feature:

⌨ *Make sure you are in the Invoice Entry window (Transactions ➔ Sales ➔ Invoice Entry).*

⌨ *Click the Trade Discount box in the lower left corner of the window. Next, click the Help menu and then click the menu option "About This Item".*

A Help window appears describing what the Trade Discount box is used for and how to enter information into it. Notice that there is another Help window beneath the Trade Discount Help window.

⌨ *Close the Trade Discount Help window to view the Help window behind it.* The other Help window is for the entire Invoice Entry window. The Overview tab is now displayed, which describes the window in general terms.

⌨ *Click the Fields tab.* This tab lists all of the description fields and boxes in the Invoice Entry window. Observe that each item is underlined and in a different color, indicating that it is a link to other related information.

⌨ *Click the "Amount Received" link.* Notice that this accesses a Help window about the Amount Received box.

⌨ *Close the Amount Received Help window.*

⌨ *Click the Messages tab.*

The Messages tab displays links to most of the common messages that you will encounter while using the Invoice Entry window. Most messages are displayed in *Dynamics* when you have made an error or when the program needs additional information.

💻 *Use the scroll box to find the message: "Do you want to add this item?" Click once on the message.* The message explains that the user tried to enter an item number that is not on file.

💻 *Close all Help windows.*

💻 *Close the Invoice Entry window.*

Opening Another Company

To switch to a different company while you are working in *Dynamics*, click the File menu and then click User and Company. Select the User ID and the new company you wish to work with.

Because the next chapter uses the sample company, Jackson Supply Company, **do not** switch companies now.

Exiting the *Dynamics* Program

Before exiting *Dynamics*, first finish working with any active windows. When you have exited all active windows, either click the Close button ☒ or click the File menu and then click Exit.

💻 *Exit the Dynamics program.*

Additional Practice

To practice some of the things you have learned so far, do the following:

💻 *Open Dynamics to the main window for Jackson Supply Company.*

💻 *Click Transactions → Purchasing → Purch. Order Entry.*

💻 *Accept Standard as the purchase order Type.*

💻 *Accept PO Number 5874.*

💻 *Use the Date box to enter the date of the purchase order, February 16, 1998.*

💻 *Select MAIN as the Default Site.*

💻 *Select the Vendor ID for Omni Incorporated.*

💻 *Accept the Name.*

💻 *Order 25 of item #113, Shampoo.*

💻 *Order 15 of item #115, Conditioner.*

You now decide to change the order for item #115 to 20 instead of 15.

🖥 *Make the change described.*

You now decide to delete item #113 entirely but retain the item #115 order (quantity is still 20). The easiest way to do that is to use the Edit menu to delete item #113 from the purchase order.

🖥 *Click any box for item #113 so that the cursor is somewhere in the entry boxes for item #113. Click the Edit menu, and then click the Delete Row option. When asked if you are sure that you want to delete this item, click Delete.*

Next, assume you find out that purchase order #5874 was voided at an earlier date, so the correct purchase order number for the Omni purchase should be #5875. Since the PO Number box cannot be edited, you will need to void the purchase order and reenter it with the correct PO number.

🖥 *Click the Void button to void the purchase order. Click Void again when asked if you are sure you want to void this record.*

🖥 *Reenter all purchase order information with the correct purchase order #5875.*

🖥 *If your window is the same as the one that follows on the next page, click the Save button to save the information.* This purchase order is saved and a blank Purchase Order Entry window appears on the screen.

Purchase Order Entry Window — Omni Incorporated

```
┌─ Purchase Order Entry ──────────────────────────────── _□X ─┐
│ ◄◄ ◄ ► ►│  [PO Number      ▼]   Save   Delete   Void        □ │
│                                                                │
│ Type            PO Number    □Q Date      品 Default Site  □Q  │
│ [Standard    ▼] 5875            2/16/98      MAIN              │
│ Vendor ID  □Q品 Name                         PO Status    Currency ID □Q品 │
│ OMNI0001        Omni Incorporated            New              │
│                                                                │
│ Item        ⓘ□Q品 U of M    Q Quantity Ordered   Unit Cost    ▤│
│ Description        Site ID □Q Quantity Canceled   Extended Cost ▤│
│ 115                1                        20              $10.75 ▲│
│ Conditioner - 50 pack  MAIN                 0             $215.00 ▒│
│                                          $0.00             $0.00 ▒│
│                                          $0.00             $0.00 ▒│
│                                                                 │
│                                                                ▼│
│ Subtotal              $215.00   Remaining PO Subtotal   $215.00 │
│ Trade Discount          $0.00                                   │
│ Freight                                                         │
│ Miscellaneous                                                   │
│ Tax                             Comment ID    □Q品               │
│ Total                 $215.00                                   │
└────────────────────────────────────────────────────────────────┘
```

🖥 *Close the Purchase Order Entry window.*

Transaction Review (Inquiry)

One of the useful features of *Dynamics* is the ease of retrieving recorded information through the Inquiry tool bar button. Transaction review is useful for evaluating whether information has been recorded correctly or to obtain information about recorded transactions or balances for customers, vendors, and management.

To demonstrate the use of transaction review, you will use the Inquiry tool bar button to review a transaction recorded in January for the sample company. This transaction has already been recorded on your data set. Complete the following:

🖥 *Click Inquiry* ➔ *Sales* ➔ *Trx by Customer.*

🖥 *Select Greenleaf Suites (GREE0001) in the Customer ID box.* Observe that two sales (SLS) and one cash receipt (PMT) have been recorded for Greenleaf.

🖥 *Highlight invoice #5127 in the scrolling window by clicking anywhere on the line containing #5127. Move the mouse pointer over the Document Number description field until the pointer turns into a magnifying glass and click once.*

The Invoice Inquiry window for invoice #5127 appears. The window is a replica of the Invoice Entry window for invoice #5127. Observe on the top of the window that you have no options for deleting or posting the transaction again. *Dynamics* provides this internal control to prevent misstatements and possible fraud.

You can inquire about additional information for such things as customer, item number sold, and tax by clicking various expansion buttons to enter other windows.

🖥 *Click the expansion button next to the Customer ID box to enter the Invoice Customer Detail Inquiry window.* Observe that the window contains information about the customer's address, contact person, payment terms, and so on. *Close this window to return to the Invoice Inquiry window.*

🖥 *Click the expansion button next to the Item Number box to enter the Invoice Item Detail Inquiry window.* Observe that the window contains information about inventory Item #101, Bath towels, including unit cost, selling price, and quantity sold. *Close this window to return to the Invoice Inquiry window.*

You can also inquire about other information using the two additional window buttons in the bottom right corner of the inquiry window.

🖥 *Click the Distributions button to enter the Invoice Distribution Inquiry window and review the account distributions for the sale to Greenleaf. Close all inquiry windows to return to the Dynamics main window.*

You can also inquire about the same information as previously shown, using the document number to find the transaction, instead of the customer ID.

⌨ *Click Inquiry ➔ Sales ➔ Trx by Document to inquire about transactions by document number.* Observe that the window includes several sales transactions and customer payments.

⌨ *Highlight invoice #5127 in the scrolling window by clicking anywhere on the line containing invoice #5127. Move the mouse pointer over the Document Number description field until the pointer turns into a magnifying glass and click once.* Observe that you have entered the same Invoice Inquiry window for invoice #5127 that you reviewed earlier. This illustrates that there are alternate ways to enter inquiry windows.

From this window, you can also open the other inquiry windows in the same manner as previously shown.

⌨ *Practice opening and closing additional inquiry windows until you feel comfortable doing so. Then return to the Receivables Transaction Inquiry – Document window.*

To obtain information about the amount still unpaid for a specific invoice, the Amount Remaining description field is used.

⌨ *Highlight invoice #5123 in the Receivables Transaction Inquiry – Document window and move the mouse pointer over the Amount Remaining description field until it turns into a magnifying glass. Click once to enter the Applied From Credits window.* Observe that the $10,347.75 invoice was paid by cash of $10,150.65 and a sales discount of $197.10. *Close all inquiry windows to return to the Dynamics main window.*

The Inquiry function is also useful to determine the aging of individual accounts receivable.

⌨ *Click Inquiry ➔ Sales ➔ Payment Summary to enter the Customer Payment Summary Inquiry window.*

⌨ *Use the Customer Lookup button to select Greenleaf Suites.* Observe that all $12,537.00 of outstanding invoices are current. *Next, close this window to return to the Dynamics main window.*

To summarize, transaction review through the Inquiry function provides the ability to obtain information about such things as recorded transactions, account balances, customers, vendors, and employees. This information is useful to determine whether a transaction has been recorded correctly, but it is also used to obtain information for management, employees, customers, and vendors. Inquiry was shown only for Sales, but the same concepts apply to all other transaction cycles.

All procedures are now complete for this chapter. Complete Chapter 3 next, where you will practice recording transactions and performing other activities using *Dynamics*.

CHAPTER 3

Practice

Introduction

In Chapter 3, you will learn how to record transactions and perform other activities commonly done in *Dynamics* by using the computer. You will use the same company that was used in Chapter 2, Jackson Supply Company, to complete Chapter 3. For each of the practice exercises summarized on the previous page, you will be provided information about a transaction or other activity and Reference book pages that provide detailed instructions to complete the practice exercise. Windows showing the correct information are provided to help your learning.

Before beginning the first practice section, you should read the introduction on pages 2-3 of the Reference book. Read the section Suggested Way to Use the Reference Book especially carefully.

You should do all fifteen practice exercises in the order listed. The knowledge you gain in Chapter 3 will be applied to Chapters 4 through 6.

If, at any time, you decide that you want to start the chapter over, you may do so by installing the *Dynamics* software again following Step 1 of the installation instructions in Chapter 1. You may want to do so if you believe that you do not understand the material in the chapter. If you install the *Dynamics* software again, all previously installed *Dynamics* software and related data files will be overwritten.

Throughout this project, 1998 has been adopted as the business activity year for purposes of demonstrating transaction entry and report generation. However, all date entry boxes in *Dynamics* default to your computer's current date or the date of the last transaction entered. Thus, you will need to pay close attention to dates to ensure that you enter the correct 1998 date. Of course, when companies process information using *Dynamics* in real time, the current date usually is the proper default date for the entry window.

Make a Credit Sale

Reference Material

A credit sale is processed through the Invoice Entry window, an example of which is shown on page 5 of the Reference book. Read and understand the Make a Credit Sale Overview on page 4 of the Reference book before processing the transaction.

Follow the instructions on pages 4-10 of the Reference book as you complete the practice section. **Recall from Chapter 2 that if a box is not mentioned in the Reference book, you do not have to do anything with that box.**

Do not be concerned about making mistakes during the practice section. These sections are for your benefit only and any errors that you make will not affect the graded assignments in later sections.

You are to record two credit sale invoices for the sample company, Jackson Supply Company. Keep in mind that you can make most corrections prior to posting the transaction by clicking the appropriate box and correcting the error.

Practice Transaction #1

Process a credit sale invoice in Dynamics using the information that follows, but do not post the invoice yet. **When you enter information for inventory items sold, make sure you move the cursor all the way to the next blank Item Number box. Otherwise, the Tax Amount box will not show the correct tax.**

- **Invoice number**: 5128
- **Date**: February 2, 1998
- **Default Site**: MAIN (Warehouse)
- **Customer Name**: The Columbus Inn
- **Customer ID**: COLU0001
- **Customer PO #**: 63921
- **Products sold**:

Item #	Qty.	Unit Price	Description	Unit Cost	Mkdown %
112	20	$72.50	Draperies	$56.00	None
116	10	$3.40	Shower cap - 25	$2.50	None

- **General ledger account information**: All default account numbers are correct.

The diagrams on page 3-6 show the Invoice Entry and Invoice Distribution Entry windows with practice transaction #1 entered.

💻 *If your windows are consistent with the diagrams, post the invoice. If there are errors, correct them before posting.*

Transaction Review

💻 *Follow the instructions on pages 9 and 10 of the Reference book to review invoice #5128. When you are done reviewing the invoice, close all inquiry windows.*

Practice Transaction #2

The second practice transaction is a bit more complicated because (1) it involves a price markdown and (2) one of the default general ledger accounts must be changed before the transaction is posted.

💻 *Process another credit sale invoice in Dynamics from the information that follows, but do not post the invoice yet.*

- **Invoice number**: 5129
- **Date**: February 10, 1998
- **Default Site**: MAIN (Warehouse)
- **Customer Name**: Oaklawn Hotel
- **Customer ID**: OAKL0001
- **Customer PO #**: PO40297
- **Products sold**:

Item #	Qty.	Unit Price	Description	Unit Cost	Mkdown %
114	30	$27.50	Bar soap - 50 pk.	$21.15	5%
117	25	$11.75	Hand lotion - 50 pk.	$9.00	None

- **General ledger account information**: All default account numbers are correct, except the price markdown portion of the transaction (Type = "MARK" in the Invoice Distribution Entry window) should be posted to A/C # 30300, Sales Discounts, instead of A/C #30100, Sales. Press the Show button to see account titles.

The diagrams on page 3-7 show the Invoice Entry and Invoice Distribution Entry windows with practice transaction #2 entered.

⌨ *If your windows are consistent with the diagrams, post the invoice. If there are errors, go back and correct them before posting.*

Transaction Review

⌨ *Follow the instructions on pages 9 and 10 of the Reference book to review invoice #5129. When you are done reviewing the invoice, close all inquiry windows.*

Error Correction After Posting the Transactions

If you discover an error after posting either invoice, refer to Appendix A in the Reference book.

Invoice Entry Window — Invoice #5128

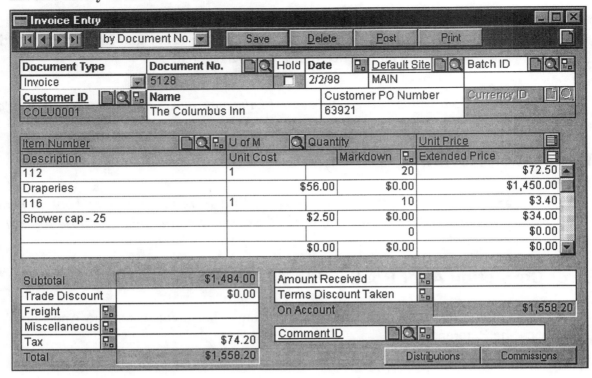

Invoice Distribution Entry — Invoice #5128

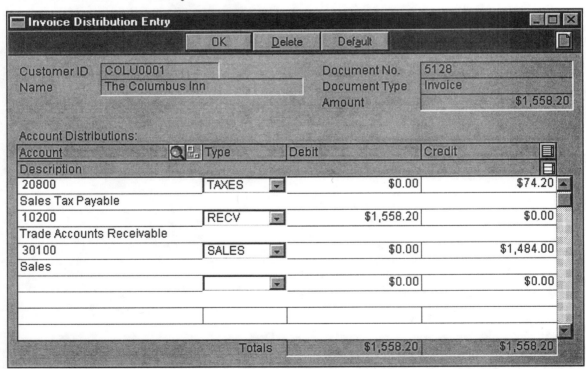

Invoice Entry Window — Invoice #5129

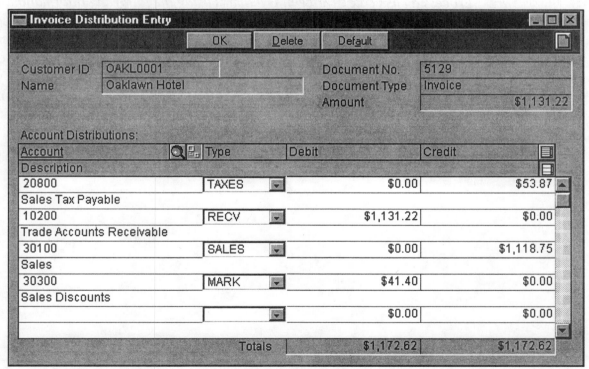

Invoice Entry

[navigation controls] | by Document No. | Save | Delete | Post | Print

Document Type	Document No.	Hold	Date	Default Site	Batch ID
Invoice	5129	☐	2/10/98	MAIN	

Customer ID	Name	Customer PO Number	Currency ID
OAKL0001	Oaklawn Hotel	PO40297	

Item Number	U of M	Quantity	Unit Price	
Description	Unit Cost	Markdown	Extended Price	
114	1	30	$27.50	
Bar soap - 50 pack	$21.15	$1.38	$783.60	
117	1	25	$11.75	
Hand lotion - 50 pack	$9.00	$0.00	$293.75	
		0	$0.00	
	$0.00	$0.00	$0.00	

Subtotal	$1,077.35
Trade Discount	$0.00
Freight	$0.00
Miscellaneous	$0.00
Tax	$53.87
Total	$1,131.22

Amount Received	$0.00
Terms Discount Taken	$0.00
On Account	$1,131.22

Comment ID

Distributions | Commissions

Invoice Distribution Entry Window — Invoice #5129

Invoice Distribution Entry

OK | Delete | Default

Customer ID	OAKL0001	Document No.	5129
Name	Oaklawn Hotel	Document Type	Invoice
		Amount	$1,131.22

Account Distributions:

Account	Type	Debit	Credit	
Description				
20800	TAXES	$0.00	$53.87	
Sales Tax Payable				
10200	RECV	$1,131.22	$0.00	
Trade Accounts Receivable				
30100	SALES	$0.00	$1,118.75	
Sales				
30300	MARK	$41.40	$0.00	
Sales Discounts				
		$0.00	$0.00	
	Totals	$1,172.62	$1,172.62	

Make a Cash Sale

Reference Material

A cash sale is processed through the Invoice Entry and Invoice Payment Entry windows, examples of which are shown on page 13 of the Reference book. In this project, all payments received are in the form of a check. In addition, the bank deposit of the check is recorded as a separate process. Read and understand the Make a Cash Sale Overview on page 12 of the Reference book and the Make a Bank Deposit Overview on page 46 of the Reference book before processing the transaction.

Follow the instructions on pages 12-18 and pages 46-48 of the Reference book as you complete the practice section. Do not be concerned about making mistakes during the practice section. These sections are for your benefit only and any errors that you make will not affect the graded assignments in later sections.

You are to practice recording a cash sale invoice for the sample company, Jackson Supply Company. Keep in mind that you can make most corrections prior to posting the transaction by clicking the appropriate box and correcting the error.

Practice Transaction

Process a cash sale invoice in Dynamics using the following information, but do not click the Insert button yet in the Invoice Payment Entry window. Only complete steps A-Q in the Quick Reference Table on page 12 of the Reference book. While entering the sale in the Invoice Entry window, make sure to move through all boxes in the scrolling window for each item sold. When you are done entering information for the last item sold, make sure the cursor is in the next blank Item Number box. The tax calculation updates for each item *after* all information for that item is entered.

- **Invoice number**: CASH549
- **Date**: February 5, 1998
- **Default Site**: MAIN (Warehouse)
- **Customer Name**: Sharon Mott
- **Customer ID**: 1000CASHCUST
- **Customer PO #**: RT98473
- **Products sold**:

Item #	Qty.	Unit Price	Description	Unit Cost	Markdown
105	15	$35.75	Queen Sheet Set	$26.50	None
110	5	$49.25	Queen Comforter	$38.00	None

- **Amount received**: Check for $821.64 (includes taxes)
- **Depository bank**: Ohio National Bank
- **Customer's check number**: 78645
- **Date of customer's payment**: February 5, 1998
- **General ledger account information**: All default account numbers are correct.

The diagram on the top of page 3-11 shows the Invoice Payment Entry window immediately *before* the Insert button is clicked (Step R). Ignore the contents of the Cash Receipt Number box in this diagram; your window may contain a different default number. These are transaction ID numbers assigned by the software and will vary from student-to-student depending upon the amount of practice done by each.

⌨ *If your Invoice Payment Entry window is consistent with the diagram (except for the Cash Receipt Number box), click the Insert button and then click the OK button to return to the Invoice Entry window. If there are errors, correct them and repeat this instruction.*

⌨ *Finish processing the cash sale in Dynamics, but do not post the invoice yet.*

The diagram on the bottom of page 3-11 shows the Invoice Entry window with the cash sale practice transaction entered. The diagram on the top of page 3-12 shows the Invoice Distribution Entry window with the proper general ledger distributions.

⌨ *If your windows are consistent with the diagrams, post the invoice. If there are errors, correct them before posting.*

⌨ *Close the Invoice Entry window.*

Make a Bank Deposit

You are to record the bank deposit for the check received from Sharon Mott.

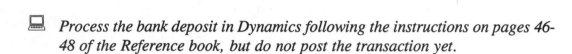 *Process the bank deposit in Dynamics following the instructions on pages 46-48 of the Reference book, but do not post the transaction yet.*

The diagram on the bottom of page 3-12 shows the Bank Deposit Entry window with the deposit completed. Ignore the contents of the Deposit Number box; your window may contain a different default number.

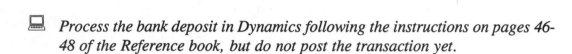 *If your window is consistent with the diagram, post the deposit. If there are errors, correct them before posting.*

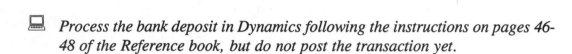 *Close the Bank Deposit Entry window.*

Transaction Review

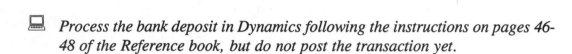 *Follow the instructions on page 18 of the Reference book to review the cash sale just posted.*

Error Correction after Posting the Transaction

If you discover an error after posting the cash sale transaction, refer to Appendix A in the Reference book.

Invoice Payment Entry Window (before Insert button is clicked)

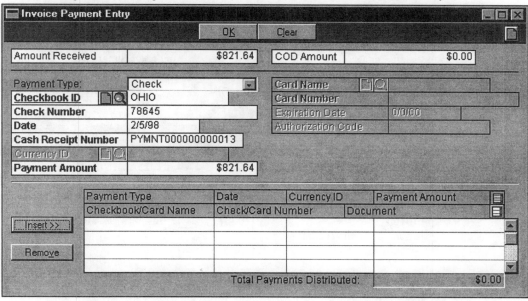

Invoice Entry Window

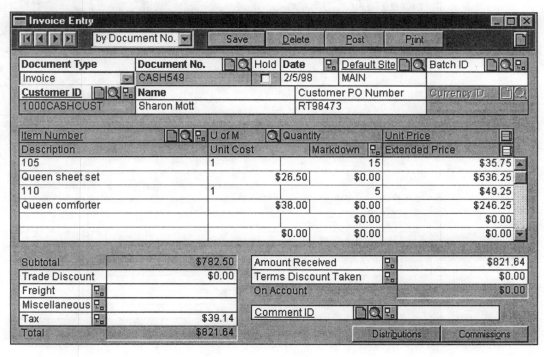

Invoice Distribution Entry Window

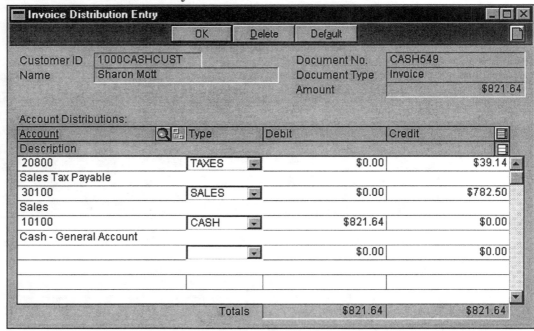

Account		Type	Debit	Credit	
Description					
20800		TAXES	$0.00	$39.14	
Sales Tax Payable					
30100		SALES	$0.00	$782.50	
Sales					
10100		CASH	$821.64	$0.00	
Cash - General Account					
			$0.00	$0.00	

Invoice Distribution Entry — OK — Delete — Default

Customer ID 1000CASHCUST   Document No. CASH549
Name Sharon Mott   Document Type Invoice
    Amount $821.64

Account Distributions:

Totals $821.64 $821.64

Bank Deposit Entry Window

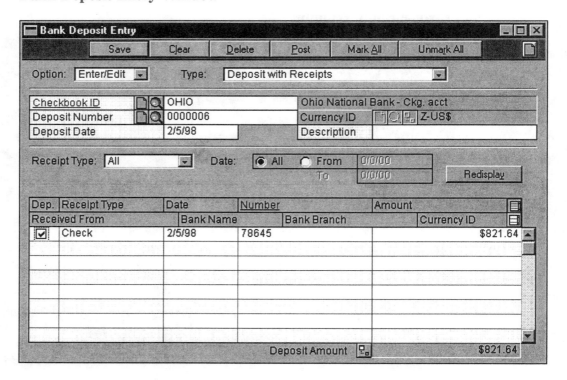

Bank Deposit Entry — Save — Clear — Delete — Post — Mark All — Unmark All

Option: Enter/Edit   Type: Deposit with Receipts

Checkbook ID OHIO   Ohio National Bank - Ckg. acct
Deposit Number 0000006   Currency ID Z-US$
Deposit Date 2/5/98   Description

Receipt Type: All   Date: ⦿ All   ○ From 0/0/00   To 0/0/00   Redisplay

Dep.	Receipt Type	Date	Number	Amount	
Received From		Bank Name	Bank Branch	Currency ID	
☑	Check	2/5/98	78645	$821.64	

Deposit Amount $821.64

Receive Goods on a Sales Return

Reference Material

A sales return is processed through the Invoice Entry window, an example of which is shown on the top of page 21 of the Reference book. A sales return is applied to outstanding invoices through the Apply Sales Documents window, an example of which is shown on the bottom of page 21 of the Reference book. Both processing and applying sales returns are necessary for each sales return transaction. Read and understand the Receive Goods on a Sales Return Overview on page 20 of the Reference book before processing the transaction.

Follow the instructions on pages 20-26 of the Reference book as you complete the practice section. Do not be concerned about making mistakes during the practice section. These sections are for your benefit only and any errors that you make will not affect the graded assignments in later sections.

You are to record a sales return for the sample company, Jackson Supply Company, and apply the sales return to an outstanding invoice. Keep in mind that you can make most corrections prior to posting the transaction by clicking the appropriate box and correcting the error.

Practice Transaction

Follow steps A-O in the Quick Reference Table on page 20 of the Reference book to record the following sales return in Dynamics, but do not post the sales return or apply it to the outstanding invoice yet. Use the following information to record the sales return.

The practice transaction is related to the February 2, 1998 credit sale to The Columbus Inn. You processed the original sale in the Make a Credit Sale practice section on pages 3-3 to 3-4 (practice transaction #1). On February 6, 1998, the customer returned some of the items purchased on invoice #5128. See the top of the following page for other details of the sales return.

- **Document number**: 1502
- **Date**: February 6, 1998
- **Default Site**: MAIN (Warehouse)
- **Customer Name**: The Columbus Inn
- **Customer ID**: COLU0001
- **Customer sales return request #**: RR5407
- **Items returned**:

Item #	Qty. Returned	Returned as	Unit Price/ Unit Cost	Description	Original Mkdown %
112	4	On Hand	$72.50/$56.00	Draperies	None
116	5	On Hand	$3.40/$2.50	Shower cap	None

- **General ledger account information**: All default account numbers are correct.

The diagrams on page 3-16 show the Invoice Entry and Invoice Distribution Entry windows with the practice sales return transaction entered.

🖥 *If your windows are consistent with the diagrams, post the sales return (step P in the Quick Reference Table). If there are errors, correct them before posting.*

🖥 *Close the Invoice Entry window (step Q).*

Apply the Sales Return

After the sales return transaction is posted, it must be applied to invoice #5128 using the Apply Sales Documents window.

🖥 *Follow steps R-X in the quick reference table on page 20 of the Reference book to apply the sales return to invoice #5128, but do not click the OK button yet.*

The diagram on the top of page 3-17 shows the Apply Sales Documents window with the sales return properly applied (without the Show button activated).

🖥 *If your window is consistent with the diagram, click the OK button (step X in the quick reference table). If there are errors, go back and correct them before clicking the OK button.*

Transaction Review

Follow the instructions on page 26 of the Reference book to review sales return #1502.

Error Correction after Posting the Transaction

If you discover an error after posting or applying the sales return transaction, refer to Appendix A in the Reference book.

Invoice Entry Window

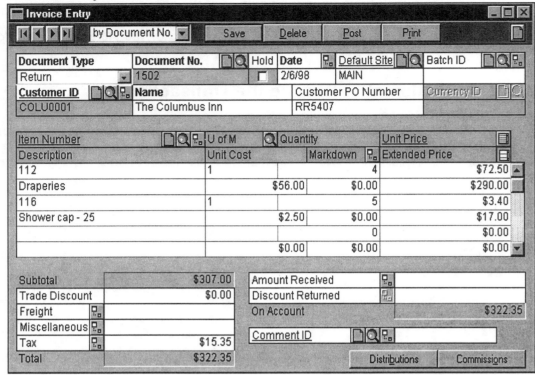

Invoice Distribution Entry Window

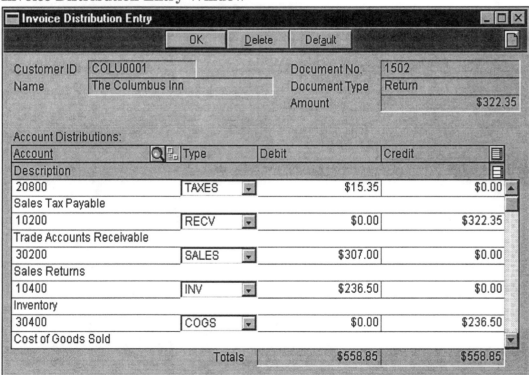

Apply Sales Documents Window

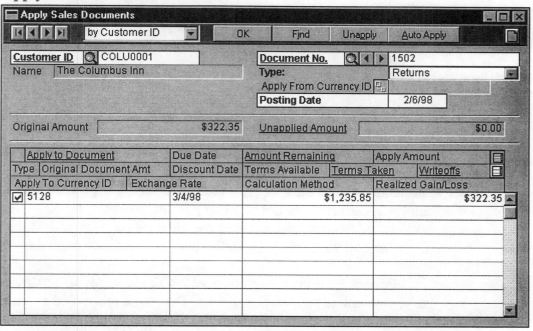

Collect an Outstanding Account Receivable

Reference Material

A collection of an account receivable is processed through the Cash Receipts Entry and Apply Sales Documents windows, examples of which are shown on page 29 of the Reference book. Similar to sales returns, the purpose of applying is to maintain the accounts receivable subsidiary records. In addition, as for cash sales, the bank deposit must be recorded as a separate process. Both processing and applying cash receipts are necessary for each collection. Read and understand the Collect an Account Receivable Overview on page 28 and Make a Bank Deposit Overview on page 46 of the Reference book before processing the transaction.

Follow the instructions on pages 28-32 and pages 46-48 of the Reference book as you complete the practice section. Do not be concerned about making mistakes during the practice section. These sections are for your benefit only and any errors that you make will not affect the graded assignments in later sections.

You are to record two account receivable collections for the sample company, Jackson Supply Company. Keep in mind that you can make most corrections prior to posting the transactions by clicking the appropriate box and correcting the error.

Practice Transaction #1

The first practice transaction illustrates an account receivable collection made within the early payment discount period.

💻 *Record practice transaction #1 in Dynamics using the following information, but do not post it yet.*

On February 1, 1998, Jackson Supply Company received a check from Greenleaf Suites in payment of invoice #5127, which was dated January 22, 1998. Jackson Supply Company's payment terms for all customers are 2%/10, Net 30.

- **Amount received**: $12,298.20 (early payment discount = $238.80)
- **Depository bank**: Ohio National Bank
- **Customer's check #**: 8421
- **General ledger account information**: All default accounts are correct.

The diagrams on page 3-21 show the Cash Receipts Entry and the Apply Sales Documents windows with the practice transaction #1 entered. Ignore the contents of the Receipt and Document No. boxes in these diagrams; your windows may contain different default numbers.

💻 *If your windows are consistent with the diagrams, post the transaction. If there are errors, correct them before posting.*

💻 *Close the Invoice Entry window.*

Make a Bank Deposit

You are to record the bank deposit for the check received from Greenleaf Suites.

💻 *Process the bank deposit in Dynamics following the instructions on pages 46-48 of the Reference book, but do not post the transaction yet.*

The diagram on the top of page 3-22 shows the Bank Deposit Entry window with the deposit completed. Ignore the contents of the Deposit Number box; your window may contain a different default number.

💻 *If your window is consistent with the diagram, post the deposit. If there are errors, correct them before posting.*

💻 *Close the Bank Deposit Entry window.*

Transaction Review

💻 *Follow the instructions on page 32 of the Reference book to review the account receivable collection transaction just posted. When you are done reviewing the transaction, close all inquiry windows.*

Practice Transaction #2

The second practice transaction is a partial payment of an outstanding invoice.

💻 *Record the account receivable collection for practice transaction #2 in Dynamics using the information that follows, but do not post the transaction yet.*

On February 7, 1998, McCarthy's Bed & Breakfast sent a check in partial payment of invoice #5126. The payment was outside the discount period.

- **Amount received**: $1,000
- **Depository bank**: Ohio National Bank
- **Customer's check #**: 7563
- **General ledger account information**: All default accounts are correct.

The diagrams on page 3-23 show the Cash Receipts Entry and Apply Sales Documents windows with the practice transaction #2 entered. Again, ignore the contents of the Receipt and Document No. Boxes in these diagrams.

💻 *If your windows are consistent with the diagrams, post the transaction. If there are errors, go back and correct them before posting.*

💻 *Close the Invoice Entry window.*

Make a Bank Deposit

You are to record the bank deposit for the check received from McCarthy's Bed & Breakfast.

💻 *Process the bank deposit in Dynamics following the instructions on pages 46-48 of the Reference book, but do not post the transaction yet.*

The diagram on the top of page 3-24 shows the Bank Deposit Entry window with the deposit completed. Ignore the contents of the Deposit Number box; your window may contain a different default number.

💻 *If your window is consistent with the diagram, post the deposit. If there are errors, correct them before posting.*

💻 *Close the Bank Deposit Entry window.*

Transaction Review

💻 *Follow the instructions on page 32 of the Reference book to review the account receivable collection transaction just posted. When you are done reviewing the transaction, close all inquiry windows.*

Error Correction After Posting the Transactions

If you discover an error after posting either practice transaction, refer to Appendix A in the Reference book.

Cash Receipts Entry Window — Practice Transaction #1

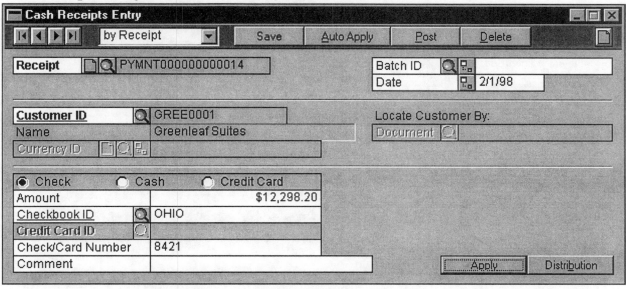

Apply Sales Documents Window — Practice Transaction #1

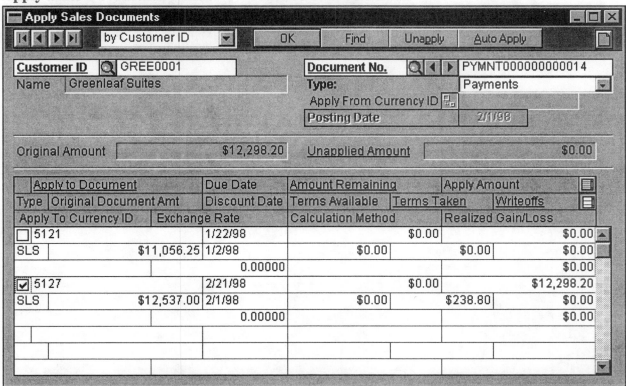

Bank Deposit Entry Window — Practice Transaction #1

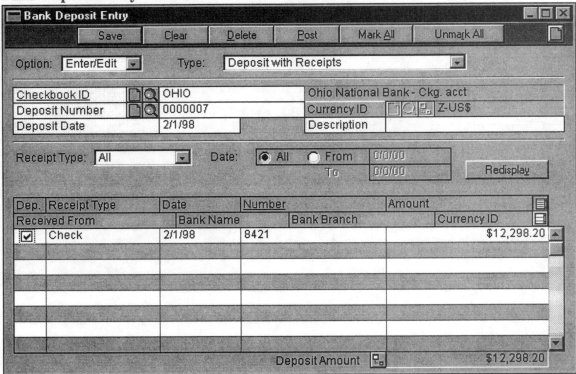

Cash Receipts Entry Window — Practice Transaction #2

Cash Receipts Entry　　　　　　　　　　_ □ ✕

| ◄◄ ◄ ► ►► | by Receipt ▼ | Save | Auto Apply | Post | Delete | 🗋 |

Receipt 🗋🔍 PYMNT000000000015

Batch ID 🔍▦
Date ▦ 2/7/98

Customer ID 🔍 MCCA0001
Name McCarthy's Bed & Breakfast
Currency ID 🗋🔍▦

Locate Customer By:
Document 🔍

◉ Check　　○ Cash　　○ Credit Card
Amount　　　　　　　　　$1,000.00
Checkbook ID 🔍 OHIO
Credit Card ID 🔍
Check/Card Number 7563
Comment

Apply　　Distribution

Apply Sales Documents Window — Practice Transaction #2

Apply Sales Documents　　　　　　　　　_ □ ✕

| ◄◄ ◄ ► ►► | by Customer ID ▼ | OK | Find | Unapply | Auto Apply | 🗋 |

Customer ID 🔍 MCCA0001
Name McCarthy's Bed & Breakfast

Document No. 🔍 ◄ ► PYMNT000000000015
Type: Payments ▼
Apply From Currency ID ▦
Posting Date 2/7/98

Original Amount $1,000.00　　Unapplied Amount $0.00

| Apply to Document | | Due Date | Amount Remaining | Apply Amount | ▤ |
| Type | Original Document Amt | Discount Date | Terms Available | Terms Taken | Writeoffs | ▤ |
Apply To Currency ID	Exchange Rate	Calculation Method	Realized Gain/Loss	
☑ 5126		2/18/98	$2,131.36	$1,000.00	▲
SLS	$3,286.50	1/29/98	$62.60	$0.00	$0.00
		0.00000		$0.00	
					▼

Bank Deposit Entry Window — Practice Transaction #2

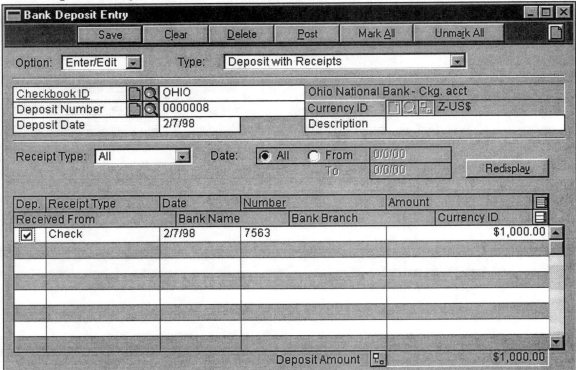

Write-off an Uncollectible Account Receivable

Reference Material

A write-off of an account receivable is processed through the Receivables Transaction Entry window, an example of which is shown on page 35 of the Reference book. Read and understand the Write-off an Uncollectible Account Receivable Overview on page 34 of the Reference book before processing the transaction.

Follow the instructions on pages 34-39 of the Reference book as you complete the practice section. Do not be concerned about making mistakes during the practice section. These sections are for your benefit only and any errors that you make will not affect the graded assignments in later sections.

You are to record a write-off of an account receivable for the sample company, Jackson Supply Company. Keep in mind that you can make most corrections prior to posting the transaction by clicking the appropriate box and correcting the error.

Practice Transaction

💻 *Process an account receivable write-off transaction in Dynamics using the following information, but do not post the transaction yet.*

McCarthy's Bed & Breakfast filed for bankruptcy protection and is unable to pay its outstanding receivable balance from invoice #5126. Recall from the previous practice section that the customer remitted $1,000.00 of the invoice balance on February 7, 1998. The remaining balance is to be written off. Other details of the write-off transaction follow:

- **Write-off date**: February 12, 1998
- **Customer ID & Name**: MCCA0001, McCarthy's Bed & Breakfast
- **Invoice written off**: #5126
- **Amount written off**: $2,131.36 (balance outstanding)
- **General ledger account information**:
  Dr. #10300 (Allowance for uncollectible accounts)
      Cr. #10200 (Trade accounts receivable)

The diagrams on the bottom of this page and on page 3-27 show the Receivables Transaction Entry, Apply Sales Documents, and Sales Transaction Distribution Entry windows with the Write-off an Account Receivable practice transaction entered. Ignore the credit memo number (CR1) in these diagrams. Your windows may contain a different default number.

⌨ *If your windows are consistent with the diagrams, post the write-off. If there are errors, correct them before posting.*

Transaction Review

⌨ *Follow the instructions on page 38-39 of the Reference book to review the write-off transaction just posted.*

Error Correction After Posting the Transaction

If you discover an error after posting the transaction, refer to Appendix A in the Reference book.

Receivables Transaction Entry Window

Apply Sales Documents Window

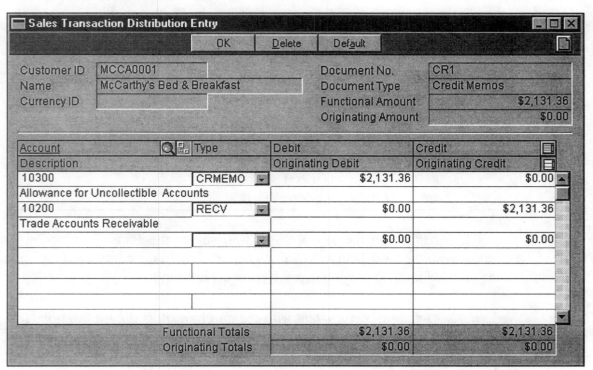

Apply Sales Documents

| by Customer ID | OK | Find | Unapply | Auto Apply |

Customer ID 🔍 MCCA0001
Name   McCarthy's Bed & Breakfast

Document No. 🔍 ◄ ► CR1
Type: Credit Memos
Apply From Currency ID
Posting Date   2/12/98

Original Amount $2,131.36   Unapplied Amount $0.00

Apply to Document		Due Date	Amount Remaining		Apply Amount	
Type	Original Document Amt	Discount Date	Terms Available	Terms Taken	Writeoffs	
Apply To Currency ID	Exchange Rate		Calculation Method		Realized Gain/Loss	
☑ 5126		2/18/98		$0.00		$2,131.36
SLS	$3,286.50	1/29/98	$0.00	$0.00		$0.00
		0.00000				$0.00

Sales Transaction Distribution Entry Window

Sales Transaction Distribution Entry

| OK | Delete | Default |

Customer ID   MCCA0001
Name   McCarthy's Bed & Breakfast
Currency ID

Document No.   CR1
Document Type   Credit Memos
Functional Amount $2,131.36
Originating Amount $0.00

Account 🔍	Type	Debit	Credit	
Description		Originating Debit	Originating Credit	
10300	CRMEMO	$2,131.36	$0.00	
Allowance for Uncollectible Accounts				
10200	RECV	$0.00	$2,131.36	
Trade Accounts Receivable				
		$0.00	$0.00	

| Functional Totals | $2,131.36 | $2,131.36 |
| Originating Totals | $0.00 | $0.00 |

Receive a Miscellaneous Cash Receipt

Reference Material

Miscellaneous cash receipts, such as loan proceeds or sales of fixed assets or marketable securities, are processed through the Bank Transaction Entry window. An example of the window is shown on page 41 of the Reference book. In addition, as for cash sales and collection of accounts receivable, the bank deposit must be recorded as a separate process. Read and understand the Receive a Miscellaneous Cash Receipt Overview on page 40 and Make a Bank Deposit Overview on page 46.

Follow the instructions on pages 40-44 and pages 46-48 of the Reference book as you complete the practice section. Do not be concerned about making mistakes during the practice section. These sections are for your benefit only and any errors that you make will not affect the graded assignments in later sections.

You are to record a miscellaneous cash receipt for a bank loan for the sample company, Jackson Supply Company. Keep in mind that you can make most corrections prior to posting the transaction by clicking the appropriate box and correcting the error.

Practice Transaction

🖳 *Process a miscellaneous cash receipt transaction in Dynamics using the following information, but do not post the transaction yet.*

On February 12, 1998, the company received a check for $5,000 from Sun Bank for a note payable that is due February 12, 2002.

> - **Depository bank**: Ohio National Bank
> - **General ledger account information**:
>   Dr. #10100 (Cash - General Account)
>   Cr. #21100 (Long-Term Debt)

The diagram on the top of page 3-30 shows the Bank Transaction Entry window with the bank loan transaction entered. Ignore the contents of the Number box; your window may contain a different default number.

🖳 *If your window is consistent with the diagram, post the transaction. If there are errors, correct them before posting.*

🖳 *Close the Bank Transaction Entry window.*

Make a Bank Deposit

You are to record the bank deposit for the check received from Sun Bank.

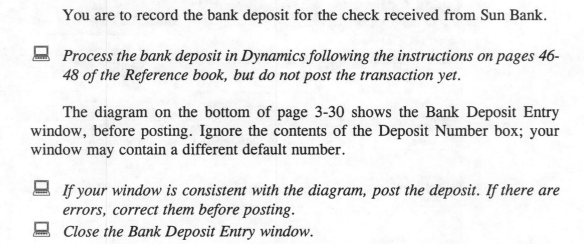 *Process the bank deposit in Dynamics following the instructions on pages 46-48 of the Reference book, but do not post the transaction yet.*

The diagram on the bottom of page 3-30 shows the Bank Deposit Entry window, before posting. Ignore the contents of the Deposit Number box; your window may contain a different default number.

If your window is consistent with the diagram, post the deposit. If there are errors, correct them before posting.

Close the Bank Deposit Entry window.

Transaction Review

Because a miscellaneous cash receipt does not affect any subsidiary records, you will not be able to review the transaction yet. Recall that the transaction has not yet been posted to the general ledger.

Error Correction After Posting the Transaction

If you discover an error after posting the miscellaneous cash receipt transaction, refer to Appendix A in the Reference book.

Bank Transaction Entry Window

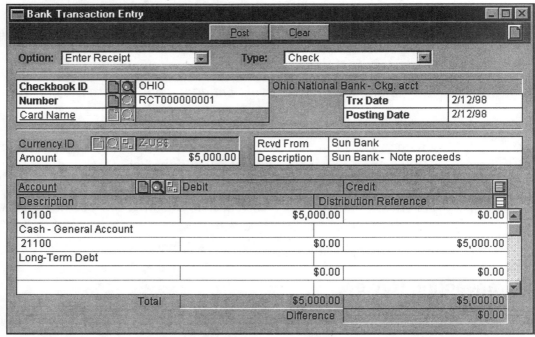

Bank Deposit Entry Window

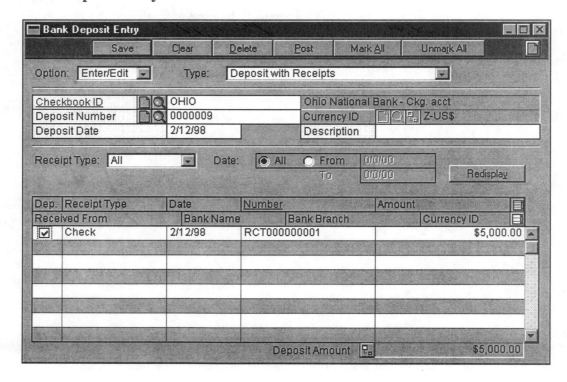

Prepare a Purchase Order

Reference Material

A purchase order is prepared through the Purchase Order Entry window, an example of which is shown on page 51 of the Reference book. Read and understand the Prepare a Purchase Order Overview on page 50 of the Reference book before processing the transaction.

Follow the instructions on pages 50-55 of the Reference book as you complete the practice section. Do not be concerned about making mistakes during the practice section. These sections are for your benefit only and any errors that you make will not affect the graded assignments in later sections.

You are to prepare two purchase orders for the sample company, Jackson Supply Company. The first purchase order is for inventory items and the second is for office equipment (non-inventory items). Keep in mind that you can make most corrections prior to saving a purchase order by clicking the appropriate box and correcting the error.

Practice Transaction #1 — Purchase Order for Inventory Items

Process the first purchase order in Dynamics using the following information, but do not save it yet.

* **PO Number:** 5876
* **Date:** February 11, 1998
* **Default Site:** MAIN (Warehouse)
* **Vendor Name:** Omni Incorporated
* **Vendor ID:** OMNI0001
* **Inventory items ordered:**

Item #	U of M	Quantity Ordered	Unit Cost	Description
114	Each	20	$21.15	Bar soap - 50 pack
117	Each	10	$ 9.00	Hand lotion - 50 pack

The diagram on the top of page 3-33 shows the Purchase Order Entry window with purchase order #5876 entered.

If your window is consistent with the diagram, save the purchase order. If there are errors, correct them before saving.

Purchase Order Review

🖳 *Follow the instructions on page 55 of the Reference book to review purchase order #5876. When you are done reviewing the purchase order, close all inquiry windows.*

Practice Transaction #2 — Purchase Order for Non-Inventory Items

On February 11, 1998, the company also ordered 10 telephone pagers that will be added to the company's fixed assets upon receipt.

🖳 *Process the second purchase order in Dynamics using the following information, but do not save it yet.* Because this transaction is for a non-inventory item; you must type Item, Quantity Ordered, Unit Cost, and Description, instead of using the Lookup button.

- **PO Number**: 5877
- **Date**: February 11, 1998
- **Default Site**: EAST (Office)
- **Vendor Name**: Standard Office Supplies
- **Vendor ID**: STAN0001
- **Office equipment ordered**:

Vendor Item #	U of M	Quantity Ordered	Unit Cost	Description
PAG-00BL	Each	10	$39.95	Pager - Black

The diagram on the bottom of page 3-33 shows the Purchase Order Entry window with purchase order #5877 entered.

🖳 *If your window is consistent with the diagram, save the purchase order. If there are errors, correct them before saving.*

Purchase Order Review

🖳 *Follow the instructions on page 55 of the Reference book to review purchase order #5877. When you are done reviewing the purchase order, close all inquiry windows.*

Error Correction after Saving the Purchase Orders

If you discover an error after saving either purchase order, refer to Appendix A in the Reference book.

Purchase Order Entry Window — PO #5876

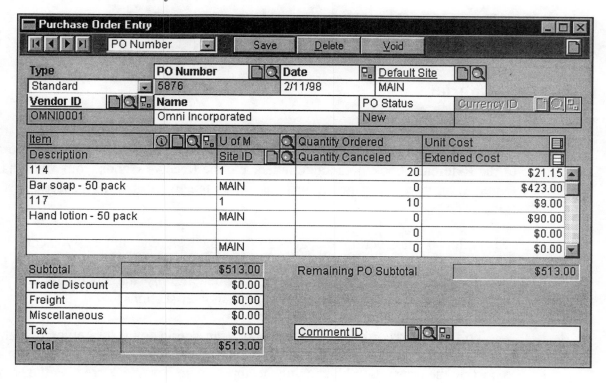

Purchase Order Entry

	PO Number							
	PO Number	Save	Delete	Void				

Type	PO Number	Date	Default Site
Standard	5876	2/11/98	MAIN

Vendor ID	Name	PO Status	Currency ID
OMNI0001	Omni Incorporated	New	

Item	U of M	Quantity Ordered	Unit Cost
Description	Site ID	Quantity Canceled	Extended Cost
114	1	20	$21.15
Bar soap - 50 pack	MAIN	0	$423.00
117	1	10	$9.00
Hand lotion - 50 pack	MAIN	0	$90.00
		0	$0.00
	MAIN	0	$0.00

Subtotal	$513.00
Trade Discount	$0.00
Freight	$0.00
Miscellaneous	$0.00
Tax	$0.00
Total	$513.00

Remaining PO Subtotal $513.00

Comment ID

Purchase Order Entry Window — PO #5877

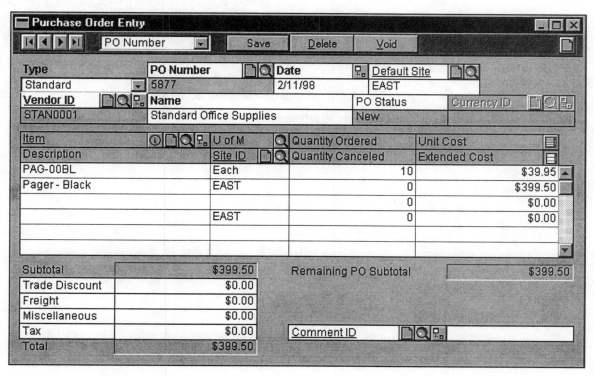

Purchase Order Entry

	PO Number							
	PO Number	Save	Delete	Void				

Type	PO Number	Date	Default Site
Standard	5877	2/11/98	EAST

Vendor ID	Name	PO Status	Currency ID
STAN0001	Standard Office Supplies	New	

Item	U of M	Quantity Ordered	Unit Cost
Description	Site ID	Quantity Canceled	Extended Cost
PAG-00BL	Each	10	$39.95
Pager - Black	EAST	0	$399.50
		0	$0.00
	EAST	0	$0.00

Subtotal	$399.50
Trade Discount	$0.00
Freight	$0.00
Miscellaneous	$0.00
Tax	$0.00
Total	$399.50

Remaining PO Subtotal $399.50

Comment ID

Receive Goods from a Purchase Order

Reference Material

The receipt of goods from a purchase order is processed through the Receivings Transaction Entry window, an example of which is shown on page 57 of the Reference book. Read and understand the Receive Goods from a Purchase Order Overview on page 56 of the Reference book before processing the transaction.

Follow the instructions on pages 56-61 of the Reference book as you complete the practice section. Do not be concerned about making mistakes during the practice section. These sections are for your benefit only and any errors that you make will not affect the graded assignments in later sections.

You are to record a receipt of goods transaction for the sample company, Jackson Supply Company. Keep in mind that you can make most corrections prior to posting the transaction by clicking the appropriate box and correcting the error.

Practice Transaction

Process a receipt of goods transaction in Dynamics using the following information, but do not post the transaction yet. You processed the purchase order in the Prepare a Purchase Order practice section on page 3-31 (practice transaction #1). **Note: Be sure to select Shipment/Invoice in the Type box or the invoice and related liability will not be recorded.**

On February 13, 1998, a *partial* shipment from purchase order #5876 is received from Omni Incorporated, along with an invoice. Other details of the transaction follow on top of the next page.

- **Vendor invoice #**: 5189
- **Goods shipped/invoiced**:

Qty. Rcvd./

Invoiced	Vendor Item #	Vendor Description	Unit Cost
20	114	Bar soap - 50 pack	$21.15

- **No trade discount, freight, miscellaneous charges, or taxes**
- **Payment terms**: 2%/10 days, Net/30
- **Invoice total (check figure)**: $423.00
- **General ledger account information**:
  Dr. A/C # 10400 (Inventory)*

      Cr. A/C # 20100 (Accounts Payable)

*   *Note: You have to enter this account since Dynamics does not show a default for this portion of the entry.*

The diagrams on page 3-36 show the Receivings Transaction Entry and the Purchasing Distribution Entry windows with the receipt from Omni Incorporated transaction entered. Ignore the contents of the Receipt Number box in both diagrams; your windows may contain a different default number.

⌨ *If your windows are consistent with the diagrams, post the transaction. If there are errors, correct them before posting.*

Transaction Review

⌨ *Follow the instructions on page 61 of the Reference book to review the receipt of goods transaction. When you are done reviewing the transaction, close all inquiry windows.*

Error Correction after Posting the Transaction

If you discover an error after posting the receipt of goods transaction, refer to Appendix A in the Reference book.

Receivings Transaction Entry Window

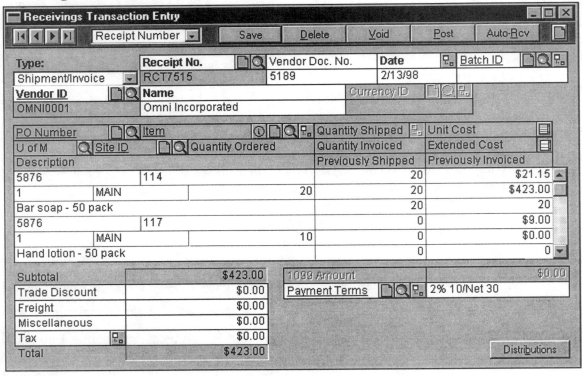

Purchasing Distribution Entry Window

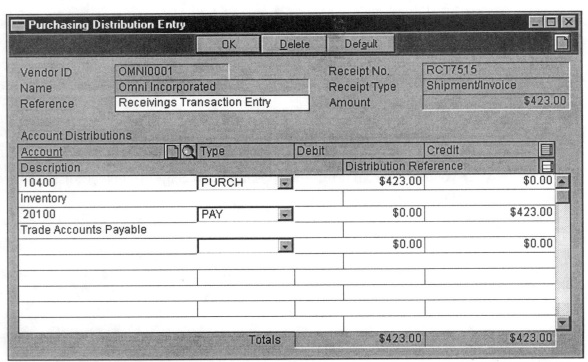

Pay a Vendor's Outstanding Invoice

Reference Material

Payment of a vendor's outstanding invoice is processed through the Payables Manual Payment Entry and Apply Payables Documents windows, examples of which are shown on page 63 of the Reference book. Read and understand the Pay a Vendor's Outstanding Invoice Overview on page 62 of the Reference book before processing the transaction.

Follow the instructions on pages 62-67 of the Reference book as you complete the practice section. Do not be concerned about making mistakes during the practice section. These sections are for your benefit only and any errors that you make will not affect the graded assignments in later sections.

You are to record a payment to one of Jackson Supply Company's vendors. Keep in mind that you can make most corrections prior to posting the transaction by clicking the appropriate box and correcting the error.

Practice Transaction

💻 *Process a cash disbursement in Dynamics using the following information, but do not post the transaction yet.*

On February 5, 1998, the company issued a check to American Linen Supply in payment of an outstanding invoice within the discount period.

- **Vendor ID**: AMER0001
- **Check number #**: 513
- **Check amount**: $9,383.50
- **Invoice paid**: #70342, totaling $9,575.00
- **Early payment discount taken**: $191.50
- **General ledger account information**:
  Dr. 20100 (Accounts Payable)
       Cr. #10100 (Cash - General Account)
       Cr. #30700 (Purchases Discounts)

The diagrams on pages 3-38 and 3-39 show the Payables Manual Payment Entry, the Apply Payables Documents, and the Payables Transaction Entry Distribution windows with the practice transaction entered. Ignore the contents of the Payment Number box in the first and last diagrams; your windows may contain a different default number.

📖 *If your windows are consistent with the diagrams, post the cash disbursement. If there are errors, correct them before posting.*

Transaction Review

📖 *Follow the instructions on page 67 of the Reference book to review the cash disbursement transaction just posted.*

Error Correction After Posting

If you discover an error after posting the cash disbursement transaction, refer to Appendix A in the Reference book.

Payables Manual Payment Entry Window

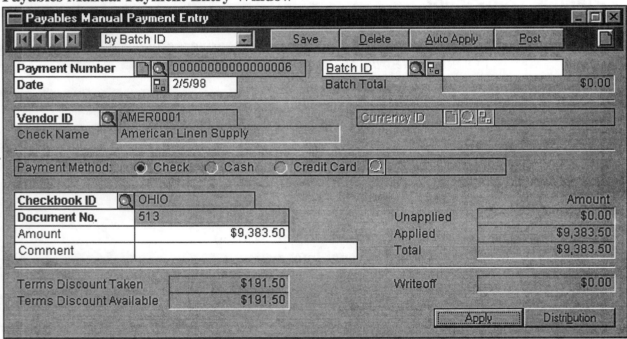

Apply Payables Documents Window

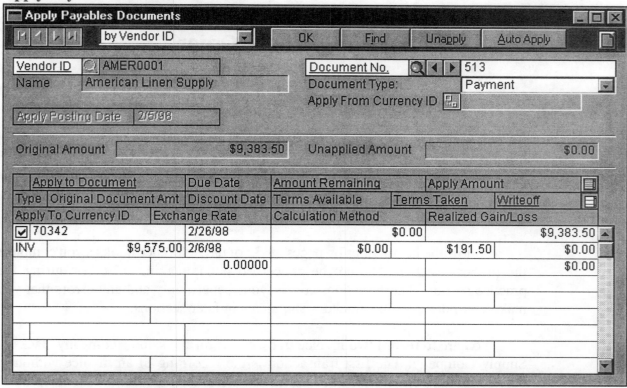

Payables Transaction Entry Distribution Window

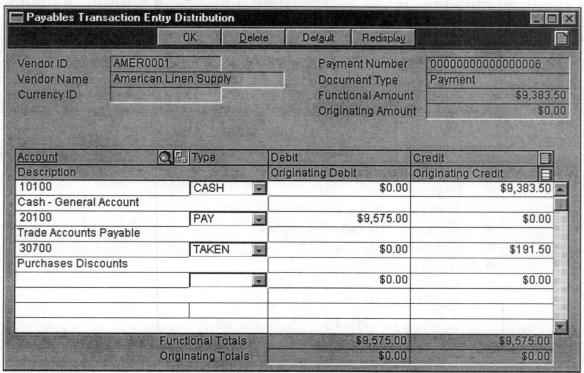

Purchase Goods or Services
Without a Purchase Order

Reference Material

A purchase of goods or services without a purchase order is processed through the Payables Transaction Entry window, an example of which is shown on page 69 of the Reference book. Read and understand the Purchase Goods or Services Without a Purchase Order Overview on page 68 of the Reference book before processing the transaction.

Follow the instructions on pages 68-73 of the Reference book as you complete the practice section. Do not be concerned about making mistakes during the practice section. These sections are for your benefit only and any errors that you make will not affect the graded assignments in later sections.

You are to record two invoice transactions for the sample company, Jackson Supply Company. The first transaction is the recording of an invoice without a corresponding payment. The second transaction is the recording of an invoice and its payment on the same date. Keep in mind that you can make most corrections prior to posting the transactions by clicking the appropriate boxes and correcting the errors.

Practice Transaction #1 — Recording an Invoice Without a Payment

Process the first vendor's invoice in Dynamics using the following information, but do not post it yet.

On February 9, 1998, Jackson Supply Company received an invoice from Miller, Roth, & Stein CPAs for tax research. Other details follow:

- **Vendor ID**: MILL0001 (Miller, Roth, Stein CPAs)
- **Payment Terms**: Net 30
- **Vendor's invoice #**: 90052
- **Shipping Method**: Not applicable
- **Amount of invoice**: $225
- **No payment made**
- **General ledger account information**:
  Dr. #41700 (Professional Fees)
      Cr. #20100 (Trade Accounts Payable)

The diagrams on page 3-43 show the Payables Transaction Entry window and the Payables Transaction Entry Distribution window with invoice #90052 entered. Ignore the contents of the Voucher No. (Number) boxes in the diagrams; your windows may contain different default numbers.

🖥 *If your windows are consistent with the diagrams, post the transaction. If there are errors, correct them before posting.*

Transaction Review

🖥 *Follow the instructions on pages 72-73 of the Reference book to review the invoice transaction just posted. When you are done reviewing the transaction, close all inquiry windows.*

Practice Transaction #2 — Recording an Invoice and a Payment on the Same Date

🖥 *Process the second invoice and its corresponding payment in Dynamics using the following information, but do not post the transaction yet.*

On February 10, 1998, Jackson Supply Company received an invoice from National Insurance Company for insurance on the company's building for the first six months of 1998. Jackson issued a check on the same day in full payment of the invoice. Other details about the invoice and payment follow:

- **Vendor ID**: NATI0001 (National Insurance Company)
- **Payment Terms**: Net 30
- **Vendor's invoice number**: 4722
- **Shipping method**: Not applicable
- **Amount of invoice**: $2,463.00
- **Payment information**:
  Ck. number: #514
  Bank: Ohio National Bank
  Check amount: $2,463.00

- **General ledger account information**:
  Dr. #41300 (Insurance)
      Cr. #10100 (Cash - General Account)

The diagrams on page 3-44 show the Payables Transaction Entry window and the Payables Transaction Entry Distribution window with the insurance invoice and payment entered. Again, ignore the contents of the Voucher No. (Number) boxes in the diagrams.

⌨ *If your windows are consistent with the diagrams, post the transaction. If there are errors, correct them before posting.*

Transaction Review

⌨ *Follow the instructions on pages 72-73 of the Reference book to review the invoice transaction just posted. When you are done reviewing the transaction, close all inquiry windows.*

Error Correction after Posting the Transactions

If you discover an error after posting either invoice transaction, refer to Appendix A in the Reference book.

Payables Transaction Entry Window — Practice Transaction #1

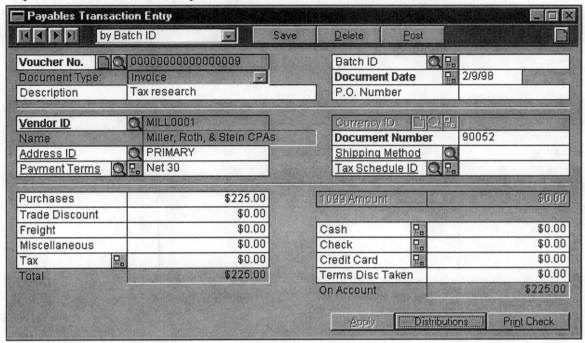

Payables Transaction Entry

by Batch ID	Save	Delete	Post	

Voucher No.	0000000000000009	Batch ID	
Document Type:	Invoice	**Document Date**	2/9/98
Description	Tax research	P.O. Number	

Vendor ID	MILL0001	Currency ID	
Name	Miller, Roth, & Stein CPAs	**Document Number**	90052
Address ID	PRIMARY	Shipping Method	
Payment Terms	Net 30	Tax Schedule ID	

Purchases	$225.00	1099 Amount	$0.00
Trade Discount	$0.00		
Freight	$0.00	Cash	$0.00
Miscellaneous	$0.00	Check	$0.00
Tax	$0.00	Credit Card	$0.00
Total	$225.00	Terms Disc Taken	$0.00
		On Account	$225.00

Apply   Distributions   Print Check

Payables Transaction Entry Distribution Window — Practice Transaction #1

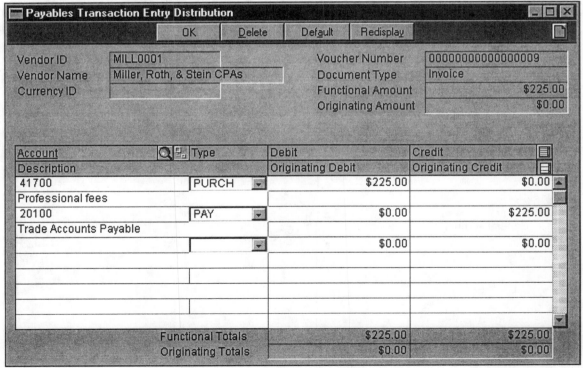

Payables Transaction Entry Distribution

OK	Delete	Default	Redisplay	

Vendor ID	MILL0001	Voucher Number	0000000000000009
Vendor Name	Miller, Roth, & Stein CPAs	Document Type	Invoice
Currency ID		Functional Amount	$225.00
		Originating Amount	$0.00

Account		Type	Debit	Credit	
Description			Originating Debit	Originating Credit	
41700		PURCH	$225.00	$0.00	
Professional fees					
20100		PAY	$0.00	$225.00	
Trade Accounts Payable					
			$0.00	$0.00	
	Functional Totals		$225.00	$225.00	
	Originating Totals		$0.00	$0.00	

Payables Transaction Entry Window — Practice Transaction #2

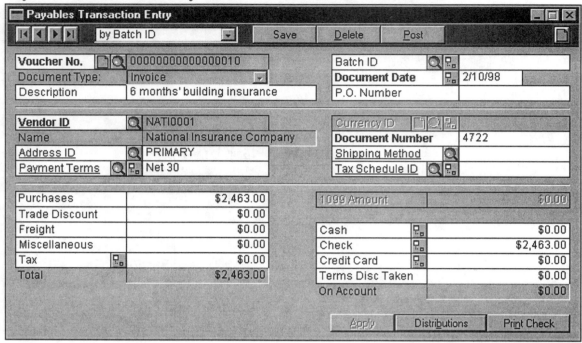

Payables Transaction Entry   _ □ ☒

| ⏮ ◀ ▶ ⏭ | by Batch ID ▼ | Save | Delete | Post | ▯ |

Voucher No.	0000000000000010	Batch ID	
Document Type:	Invoice ▾	Document Date	2/10/98
Description	6 months' building insurance	P.O. Number	

Vendor ID	NATI0001	Currency ID	
Name	National Insurance Company	Document Number	4722
Address ID	PRIMARY	Shipping Method	
Payment Terms	Net 30	Tax Schedule ID	

Purchases	$2,463.00		1099 Amount	$0.00
Trade Discount	$0.00			
Freight	$0.00		Cash	$0.00
Miscellaneous	$0.00		Check	$2,463.00
Tax	$0.00		Credit Card	$0.00
Total	$2,463.00		Terms Disc Taken	$0.00
			On Account	$0.00

| Apply | Distributions | Print Check |

Payables Transaction Entry Distribution Window — Practice Transaction #2

Payables Transaction Entry Distribution   _ □ ☒

| | OK | Delete | Default | Redisplay | ▯ |

Vendor ID	NATI0001	Voucher Number	0000000000000010
Vendor Name	National Insurance Company	Document Type	Invoice
Currency ID		Functional Amount	$2,463.00
		Originating Amount	$0.00

Account	Type	Debit	Credit	
Description		Originating Debit	Originating Credit	
41300	PURCH ▾	$2,463.00	$0.00	▲
Insurance				
10100	CASH ▾	$0.00	$2,463.00	
Cash - General Account				
	▾	$0.00	$0.00	
				▼
Functional Totals		$2,463.00	$2,463.00	
Originating Totals		$0.00	$0.00	

Pay Employees

Reference Material

A payroll transaction is processed through the Payroll Manual Check Adjustment Entry - USA window and the Payroll Manual Check Transaction Entry - USA window, examples of which are shown on page 75 of the Reference book. Read and understand the Pay Employees Overview on page 74 of the Reference book before processing the transaction.

Follow the instructions on pages 74-79 of the Reference book as you complete the practice section. Do not be concerned about making mistakes during the practice section. These sections are for your benefit only and any errors that you make will not affect the graded assignments in later sections.

You are to record a semi-monthly payroll check for one of the employees of the sample company, Jackson Supply Company. Keep in mind that you can make most corrections prior to posting the transaction by clicking the appropriate box and correcting the error.

Practice Transaction

Record a payroll transaction in Dynamics using the following information, but do not post the transaction yet.

- **Employee Name**: Kenneth Jorgensen
- **Employee ID**: 10002
- **Check date and posting date**: February 11, 1998
- **Check number**: 515
- **Pay period**: 1-29-98 to 2-11-98 (bi-weekly pay period)
- **Gross pay (Code = Hour)**: $1,245.00
- **Federal income tax withholding (Transaction Type = Federal Tax)**: $100.55
- **FICA withholding (Transaction Type = FICA/Soc. Sec. Tax)** : $95.24
- **Net pay (check amount)**: $1,049.21

The diagram on the bottom of page 3-46 shows the Payroll Manual Check - Adjustment Entry - USA window with the previous transaction entered.

If your window is consistent with the diagram, post the payroll transaction. If there are errors, correct them before posting. If there is an error in a Payroll Manual Check Transaction Entry - USA window for gross pay or withholdings, refer to the instructions on page 78 of the Reference book.

Transaction Review

📖 *Follow the instructions on page 79 of the Reference book to review the payroll transaction just posted.*

Error Correction after Posting the Transaction

If you discover an error after posting the payroll transaction, refer to Appendix A in the Reference book.

Payroll Manual Check - Adjustment Entry - USA Window

Payroll Manual Check-Adjustment Entry - USA	_ □ X

| ◄◄ ◄ ► ►► | Save | Clear | Delete | Post | 🗋 |

Check Type: ● Manual Check   ○ Adjustment   ○ Beginning Balances
Payment Number 🗋🔍   7

| Batch ID 🔲🔍 | | Checks | |
| Comment | | | |

Checkbook ID 🔍 OHIO
Name   Ohio National Bank - Ckg. acct
Check Number   515
Check Date   2/11/98
Posted Date   2/11/98

Employee ID 🔍 10002
Name   Jorgensen, Kenneth J.

Gross Amount $1,245.00
Net Amount $1,049.21   Transactions

Prepare a General Journal Entry

Reference Material

A general journal entry is posted through the Transaction Entry window, an example of which is shown on page 81 of the Reference book. Read and understand the Prepare a General Journal Entry Overview on page 80 of the Reference book before processing the transaction.

Follow the instructions on pages 80-84 of the Reference book as you complete the practice section. Do not be concerned about making mistakes during the practice section. These sections are for your benefit only and any errors that you make will not affect the graded assignments in later sections.

You are to record a general journal entry for the sample company, Jackson Supply Company. Keep in mind that you can make most corrections prior to posting the journal entry by clicking the appropriate boxes and correcting the errors.

Practice Transaction

⌨ *Record a journal entry in Dynamics using the following information, but do not post it yet.*

On February 28, 1998, Jackson Supply Company records its monthly depreciation entry. For simplicity, the entry only involves recording the monthly depreciation on the building.

- **Transaction Date**: February 28, 1998
- **Monthly depreciation amount**: $1,033.00
- **General ledger accounts used**:

Name	A/C #
Depreciation - Building	40400
Accumulated Depreciation - Building	10900

The diagram on the bottom of page 3-48 shows the Transaction Entry window with the depreciation adjusting entry entered. Ignore the contents of the Journal Entry box in the diagram; your window may contain a different default number.

⌨ *If your window is consistent with the diagram, post the journal entry. If there are errors, correct them before posting.*

Journal Entry Review

💻 *Follow the instructions on page 84 of the Reference book to review the journal entry just posted. When you are done reviewing the journal entry, close all inquiry windows.*

Error Correction after Posting the Journal Entry

If you discover an error after posting the journal entry, refer to Appendix A in the Reference book.

Transaction Entry Window

Transaction Entry			
◀◀ ◀ ▶ ▶▶ by Batch ID ▼	Save	Delete	Post

Journal Entry	49	Batch ID	

Transaction Type:
⦿ Standard ○ Reversing

Transaction Date 2/28/98
Reversing Date

Source Document	GJ
Reference	February depreciation
Currency ID	

Account	Debit	Credit
Description		
Distribution Reference		
40400	$1,033.00	$0.00
Depreciation - Building		
10900	$0.00	$1,033.00
Accumulated Depreciation - Building		
Total	$1,033.00	$1,033.00
Difference		$0.00

Adjust Perpetual Inventory Records

Reference Material

An adjustment of the perpetual inventory records to equal the physical count is processed through the Item Transaction Entry window, an example of which is shown on page 87 of the Reference book. Read and understand the Adjust Perpetual Inventory Records Overview on page 86 of the Reference book before processing the transaction.

Follow the instructions on pages 86-90 of the Reference book as you complete the practice section. Do not be concerned about making mistakes during the practice section. These sections are for your benefit only and any errors that you make will not affect the graded assignments in later sections.

You are to record an adjustment of the perpetual inventory records for the sample company, Jackson Supply Company. Keep in mind that you can make most corrections prior to posting the transaction by clicking the appropriate box and correcting the error.

Practice Transaction

Record an adjustment to the perpetual inventory records in Dynamics using the following information, but do not post the transaction yet.

On February 28, 1998, a physical inventory count was taken by company personnel. There were differences between the physical count and the perpetual quantities recorded in *Dynamics* for two inventory items. The physical count is the correct quantity for both items.

		Qty. per physical count	Qty. per perpetual records
•	**Date of adjustment of the perpetual records**: February 28, 1998		
•	**Default Site ID**: MAIN (Warehouse)		
•	**Details of differences**:		
Item #	Description		
102	Hand towels - 100 pack	125	120
113	Shampoo - box of 50	359	361
•	**All default general ledger account distributions are correct.**		

The diagram at the bottom of this page shows the Item Transaction Entry window with the adjustment of the perpetual inventory records transaction entered. Ignore the contents of the Number box in the diagram.

If your window is consistent with the diagram, post the transaction. If there are errors, correct them before posting.

Transaction Review

Follow the instructions on pages 89-90 of the Reference book to review the transaction just posted. When you are done reviewing the transaction, close all inquiry windows.

Error Correction After Posting the Transaction

If you discover an error after posting the adjustment to the perpetual records, refer to Appendix A in the Reference book.

Item Transaction Entry Window

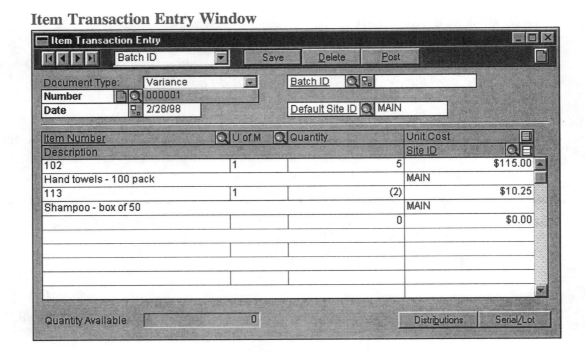

Prepare a Bank Reconciliation

Reference Material

A bank reconciliation is prepared through the Reconcile Bank Statements window, an example of which is shown on page 93 of the Reference book. Read and understand the Prepare a Bank Reconciliation Overview on page 92 of the Reference book before processing the transaction.

Follow the instructions on pages 92-100 of the Reference book as you complete the practice section. Do not be concerned about making mistakes during the practice section. These sections are for your benefit only and any errors that you make will not affect the graded assignments in later sections.

You are to prepare the bank reconciliation for the month of January 1998 for the sample company, Jackson Supply Company. The transactions processed in this chapter do not affect the bank reconciliation because they are all in February, whereas the bank reconciliation is as of January 31, 1998. Keep in mind that you can make most corrections prior to reconciling the bank statement by clicking the appropriate box and correcting the error.

Practice Activity

📖 *Prepare the January bank reconciliation in Dynamics through step E in the Quick Reference Table on page 92 of the Reference book, using the following information.* **CAUTION: Do not click the Transactions button in the Reconcile Bank Statements window until you are told to in the instructions on page 3-52.**

- **Checkbook ID**: OHIO (Ohio National Bank)
- **Bank Statement Ending Balance**: $18,119.07
- **Bank Statement Ending Date**: January 31, 1998
- **Cutoff Date**: January 31, 1998
- **Deposits in transit**: None
- **Checks not clearing the bank (outstanding checks)**:

Ck. #	Amount
506	$ 392.00
510	$1,672.89
511	$1,011.28
512	$ 556.58

- **Service charge on bank statement, not yet recorded in G/L**: $31.50
- **G/L posting account for service charge**: A/C #41800, Miscellaneous

---

The diagram on the top of page 3-53 shows the Reconcile Bank Statements window before the Transactions button is clicked.

💻 *If your window is consistent with the diagram, click the Transactions button to open the Select Bank Transactions window. If there are errors in the Reconcile Bank Statements window, correct them before clicking the Transactions button.*

💻 *Continue preparing the January bank reconciliation in Dynamics through step O in the Quick Reference Table, but do not click the OK button yet in the Reconcile Bank Adjustments window.*

The diagram on the bottom of page 3-53 shows the Reconcile Bank Adjustments Window *before* the OK button is clicked. Ignore the default service charge number; your window may contain a different default number.

💻 *If your window is consistent with the diagram, click the OK button to return to the Select Bank Transactions window. If there are errors, correct them before continuing.*

The diagram on page 3-54 shows the Select Bank Transactions window with the correct information entered, but before the Reconcile button is clicked.

💻 *If your window is consistent with the diagram, click the Reconcile button. If there is an error, you must correct it before clicking the Reconcile button. After the Reconcile button has been clicked, you cannot return to the bank reconciliation to correct errors.*

Bank Reconciliation Review

💻 *Follow the instructions on page 99 of the Reference book to review the bank reconciliation. When you are done reviewing the bank reconciliation, close all inquiry windows.*

Error Correction after Reconciling the Bank Statement

As stated in the previous section, you cannot return to a completed bank reconciliation to correct errors. Therefore, it is extremely important to review the bank reconciliation before clicking the Reconcile button. If a wrong general ledger account number was entered for a bank adjustment in the Reconcile Bank Adjustments window, but all other parts of the bank reconciliation are correct, you can correct the error by recording a general journal entry.

Reconcile Bank Statements Window

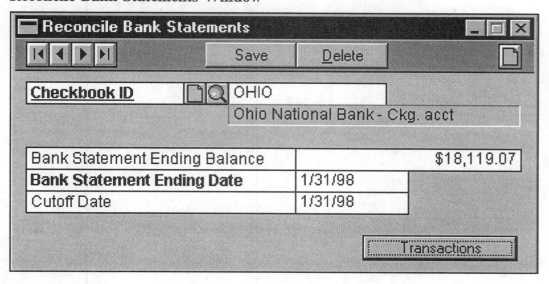

Reconcile Bank Adjustments Window

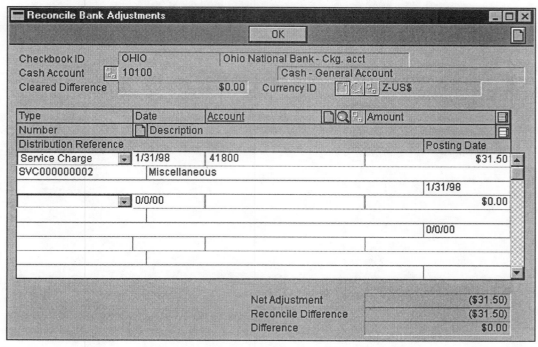

Select Bank Transactions Window

	Select Bank Transactions							_ □ X
	OK		Reconcile				▯

Checkbook ID OHIO   Display: All ▾   Sort: by Type ▾   Redisplay

Type	Number	Date	C	Payment	🖳	Deposit	🖳
DEP	0000001	1/9/98	☑	$0.00		$1,559.17	▲
DEP	0000002	1/13/98	☑	$0.00		$10,788.54	
DEP	0000003	1/20/98	☑	$0.00		$1,089.38	
DEP	0000004	1/21/98	☑	$0.00		$11,056.25	
DEP	0000005	1/23/98	☑	$0.00		$22,213.01	
CHK	501	1/2/98	☑	$14,063.00		$0.00	
CHK	502	1/8/98	☑	$1,502.00		$0.00	
CHK	503	1/14/98	☑	$1,672.89		$0.00	
CHK	504	1/14/98	☑	$1,011.28		$0.00	
CHK	505	1/14/98	☑	$556.58		$0.00	
CHK	506	1/16/98	☐	$392.00		$0.00	▼

Cleared Transactions

	No. of	Total Amount		Adjusted Bank Balance	$14,486.32
				Adjusted Book Balance	$14,486.32
Payments	8	$43,452.90		Difference 🖳	$0.00
Deposits	5	$46,706.35			

Adjustments

Perform Maintenance Activities

Maintenance Overview

When a transaction is recorded in a *Dynamics* window, one of the most useful features of the program is the default information stored in the system. For example, after a Customer ID is selected in the Invoice Entry window for a credit sale, *Dynamics* automatically completes many areas of the window, such as the customer's name and address, and the general ledger sales account for sales to that customer.

Default information is stored in the system through maintenance. There are five maintenance windows, and for each type there are three possible maintenance tasks that can be performed with the window. These are as follows:

Five Maintenance Windows
1. Customer Maintenance
2. Vendor Maintenance
3. Account Maintenance (general ledger account)
4. Employee Maintenance
5. Item Maintenance (inventory)

Three Types of Maintenance Tasks
1. Add a new record
2. View and change information in an existing record
3. Delete a record

Maintenance tasks have no effect on transactions already recorded, but certain types of maintenance tasks affect the amounts recorded in subsequent transactions. For example, changing an inventory item's cost and selling price has no effect on previously recorded sales transactions, but it will affect the amount of sales revenue and cost of goods sold posted to the general ledger for future sales of the item.

Reference Material

All maintenance tasks are processed through one or more of the five maintenance windows listed above. The reference information for maintenance is summarized on pages 102-103 of the Reference book. Read and understand the Perform Maintenance Activities Overview on page 102 of the Reference book before practicing maintenance.

Instructions for using each of the five maintenance windows to perform the three types of maintenance tasks are on pages 102-123 of the Reference book. The reference material for maintenance is less detailed than for the other reference sections because there is a wider variety of information that may or may not be entered or changed in each window.

In this section, you will practice working with each of the five types of maintenance windows shown in the Reference book. Do not be concerned about making mistakes during the practice section. These sections are for your benefit only and any errors that you make will not affect the graded assignments in later sections.

Practice Transactions

As discussed above and in the Reference book, maintenance windows are used to (1) add a new record, (2) view and change information in an existing record, and (3) delete a record. You will first practice each of these tasks using the Customer Maintenance window.

Maintenance Practice Task #1 — Add a New Customer Record

When a company obtains a new customer, a new record must be created in *Dynamics*. During this part of the practice section, you are to add a new customer record for the sample company, Jackson Supply Company, using the Customer Maintenance window.

💻 *Add a new customer record for The Wooden Shoe Inn using the Reference book instructions on page 104 and the information below, but do not save the new record yet.*

Note: All default information is correct for the new customer unless otherwise noted below. Also remember that not all boxes in the Customer Maintenance and related windows are applicable to this customer.

Customer ID:	WOOD0001
Name:	The Wooden Shoe Inn
Class ID:	SMALL (Hotels less than 100 rooms)
Address ID:	PRIMARY
Contact:	Roger Nelson
Address:	561 Lancaster
	Holland, MI 49424
Phone:	555-701-1000
Fax:	555-701-7254
Payment terms:	Net 30
G/L posting	
account change:	Writeoffs: #40900 - Bad Debt Expense
	(all other default accounts are correct)
Credit limit:	$7,500 (Use the Customer Maintenance Options window to enter)

The diagrams on pages 3-59 and 3-60 show the completed Customer Maintenance, Customer Account Maintenance, and Customer Maintenance Options windows for the Wooden Shoe Inn.

🖥 *If the windows on your screen are consistent with the diagrams, save the new customer record. If there are errors, correct them before saving the record.*

If you want to correct information after saving the new customer record, you can change the information as described in the next section.

Maintenance Practice Task #2 — Change Information in an Existing Customer Record

Often, it is necessary to change information in an existing customer's record. Examples include changing a customer's address and changing the default general ledger accounts for a customer. Edits to existing records are made using the Customer Maintenance window.

🖥 *Change the customer record for Sunway Suites using the Reference book instructions on page 107 and the following information, but do not save the revised record yet.*

Sunway Suites, an existing customer, added a second phone line with the phone number 614-897-5000. In addition, Sunway Suites is experiencing credit problems and Jackson Supply Company's management no longer wants to extend credit to the customer. *Note that the change in credit policy for Sunway must be entered using the Credit Limit radio buttons in the Customer Maintenance Options window.*

The diagrams on page 3-61 show the revised Customer Maintenance and Customer Maintenance Options windows for Sunway Suites.

🖥 *If the windows on your screen are consistent with the diagrams, save the revised customer record. If there are errors, correct them before saving the record.*

Maintenance Practice Task #3 — Delete a Customer Record

It is often desirable to remove an existing customer record from *Dynamics*. An example is a customer to which the company no longer sells goods or services.

⌨ *Delete Traver's Bed & Breakfast, Customer ID TRAV0001, using the Reference book instructions on page 107.*

⌨ *Click the Customer ID lookup button. Notice that Traver's Bed & Breakfast no longer exists in the list of customers. If the customer is still listed, select it again and repeat the steps to delete the record for Traver's Bed & Breakfast.*

Jackson Supply Company is no longer planning to do business with an existing customer, Ameristay International (Customer ID AMER0001). Practice deleting the customer record using the Customer Maintenance window as follows:

⌨ *Attempt to delete Ameristay International's customer record using the Reference book instructions on page 107.*

A warning message appears saying that you cannot delete this record because there are existing transactions for the customer. Transactions and balances from an existing customer must be cleared before *Dynamics* will allow that customer to be deleted.

⌨ *Click the OK button.*

⌨ *Close the Customer Maintenance window.*

Customer Maintenance Window — The Wooden Shoe Inn

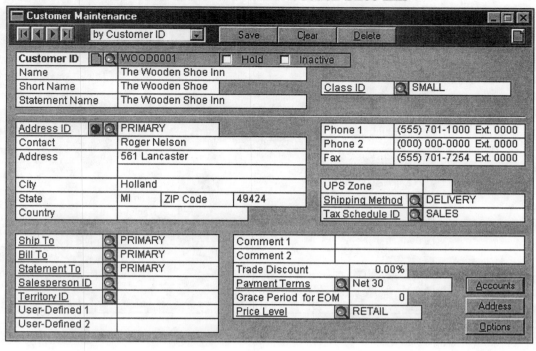

Customer Account Maintenance Window — The Wooden Shoe Inn

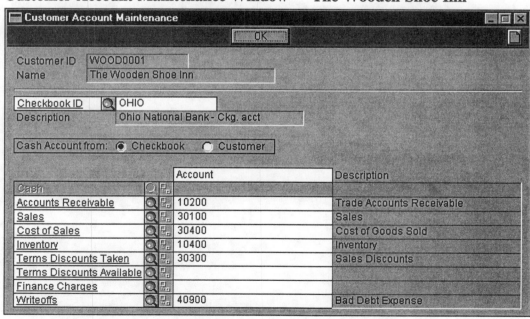

Customer Maintenance Options Window — The Wooden Shoe Inn

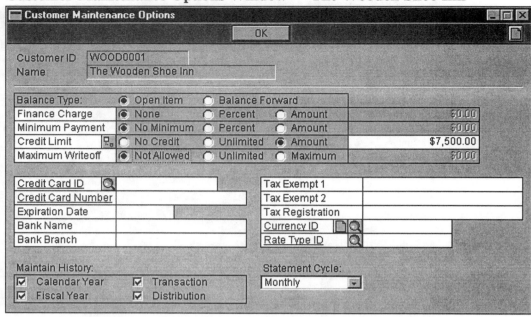

Customer Maintenance Window — Sunway Suites

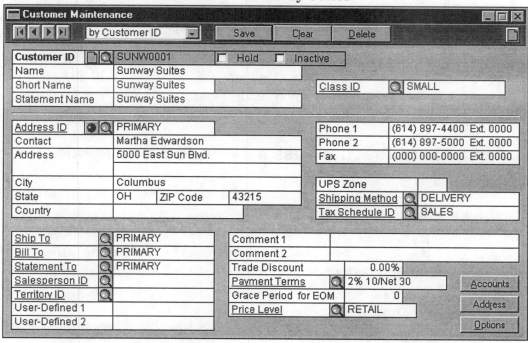

Customer Maintenance Options Window — Sunway Suites

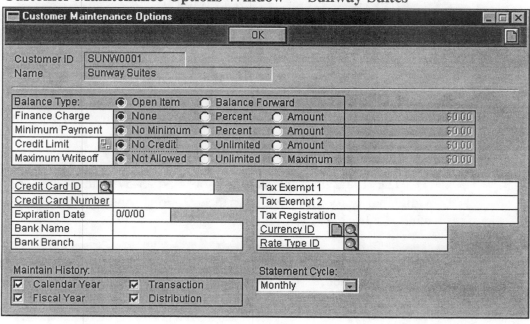

After completing maintenance practice tasks #1-3, you have practiced performing all three types of maintenance tasks with one of the five maintenance windows — Customer Maintenance. Next, you will complete maintenance tasks with the four remaining maintenance windows: Vendor Maintenance, Account Maintenance, Employee Maintenance - USA, and Item Maintenance.

Maintenance Practice Task # 4 — Add a New Vendor Record

Jackson Supply Company has a new vendor from which it purchases inventory, XYZ Warehouse.

💻 *Add a new vendor record for XYZ Warehouse using the Reference book instructions on page 108 and the information below, but do not save the new record yet.*

Note: All default information is correct for the vendor unless otherwise noted below. Also remember that not all boxes in the Vendor Maintenance and related windows are applicable to this vendor.

Vendor ID:	XYZW0001
Name:	XYZ Warehouse
Class ID:	ROOM (Room supply vendor)
Address ID:	PRIMARY
Contact:	Theresa Anthony
Address:	500 Westland Park Dr.
	Upper Saddle River, NJ 07458
Phone:	201-235-0039
Fax:	201-234-9002
Ship. method:	DELIVERY
Vendor account:	85792
Payment terms:	Net 30 (Use the Vendor Maintenance Options window to enter)
G/L accounts:	All default general ledger accounts are correct for this vendor

The diagrams on pages 3-66 and 3-67 show the completed Vendor Maintenance, Vendor Maintenance Options, and Vendor Account Maintenance windows for XYZ Warehouse.

💻 *If the windows on your screen are consistent with the diagrams, save the new vendor record. If there are errors, correct them before saving the record.*
💻 *Close the Vendor Maintenance window.*

Because changing or deleting a vendor's record is similar to changing or deleting a customer's record (practice tasks #2 and #3), no practice exercises for changing or deleting a vendor's record are considered necessary.

Maintenance Practice Task #5 — Add a General Ledger Account

The next maintenance task is to add a new general ledger account for Jackson Supply Company.

💻 *Add a new general ledger account record using the Reference book instructions on page 112 and the information below, but do not save the new record yet.*

Account Number:	20210
Description:	401K Deductions Payable
Category:	Other Current Liabilities
Posting Type:	Balance Sheet
Typical Balance:	Credit

The diagram on the bottom of page 3-67 shows the completed Account Maintenance window for the new general ledger account.

💻 *If the window on your screen is consistent with the diagram, save the new record. If there are errors, correct them before saving the record.*
💻 *Close the Account Maintenance window.*

Changing or deleting an existing general ledger account is relatively simple when you follow the instructions on page 114 of the Reference book. No practice exercises are considered necessary.

Further, in the remaining two maintenance tasks, you will practice only one of the three types of maintenance that are available in each Maintenance window. With the help of the Reference book instructions for Maintenance, you should have no difficulty with any of the other maintenance types for the two remaining maintenance windows, Employee Maintenance and Inventory Item Maintenance.

Maintenance Practice Task #6 — Increase an Employee's Pay Rate

The sample company, Jackson Supply Company, increased the hourly and overtime pay rates for Mark Phelps, an employee.

💻 *Change Mr. Phelps' employee record to reflect his increased hourly pay rate (Pay Code = HOUR), using the Reference book instructions on page 119 and the information below, but do not click the Save button yet.*

Employee ID:	10003 (Mark Phelps)
Pay Codes to be changed:	HOUR (hourly), OVER (overtime)
Old hourly rates:	$8.50 hourly, $12.75 overtime
New hourly rates:	$9.00 hourly, $13.50 overtime

The diagram on the top of page 3-68 shows the revised Employee Pay Code Maintenance - USA window for Mr. Phelps' HOUR (hourly) Pay Code.

💻 *If the window on your screen is consistent with the diagram, click the Save button to save the hourly pay rate increase. If there are errors, correct them before saving.*

💻 *After you change the hourly rate and save the information, Dynamics asks if you want this change rolled down to other pay codes that are based on the hourly pay code. Click "No".*

💻 *Next, change Mr. Phelps' employee record to reflect his increased overtime pay rate (Pay Code = OVER), using the Reference book instructions on pages 119, but do not click the Save button yet.*

The diagram on the bottom of page 3-68 shows the revised Employee Pay Code Maintenance - USA window for Mr. Phelps' OVER (overtime) Pay Code.

💻 *If the window on your screen is consistent with the diagram, click the Save button to save the overtime pay rate increase. If there are errors, correct them before saving.*

💻 *Close the Employee Pay Code Maintenance - USA window to return to the Employee Maintenance - USA window.*

💻 *Click the Save button to save the revised employee record.*

💻 *Close the Employee Maintenance - USA window.*

Maintenance Practice Task #7 — Change an Inventory Item's Cost and Selling Price

The final maintenance task is to edit an inventory item's record for changes in the item's cost and selling price.

🖥 *Change the inventory item record for item #103 using the Reference book instructions on page 123 and the information on the following page, but do not save the revised record yet.*

Item Number:	103
Description:	Washcloths - 100 pack
Old Current Cost:	$85.00
New Current Cost:	$87.00
Old List Price:	$110.50
New List Price:	$113.00

The diagram on the top of page 3-69 shows the revised Item Maintenance window for item #103. Ignore the contents of the Quantity on Hand and Quantity Available boxes; your window may contain different quantities.

🖥 *If the window on your screen is consistent with the diagram, save the revised inventory item record. If there are errors, correct them before saving the record.*

🖥 *Close the Item Maintenance window.*

Now that you have completed Chapter 3, read the Chapter Summary on page 3-70.

Vendor Maintenance Window — XYZ Warehouse

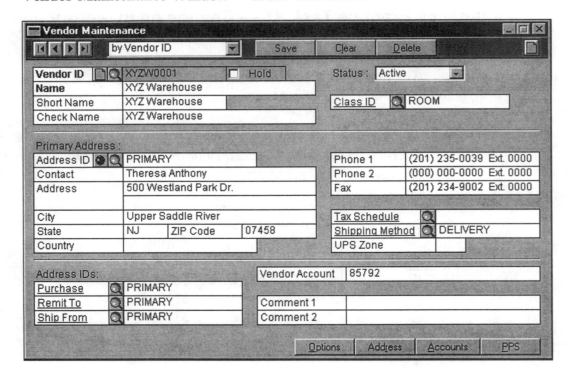

Vendor Maintenance Options Window — XYZ Warehouse

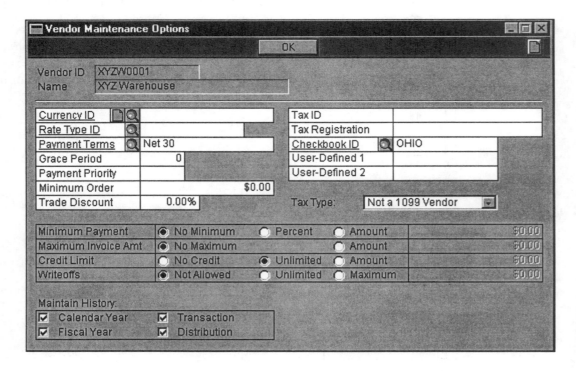

Vendor Account Maintenance Window — XYZ Warehouse

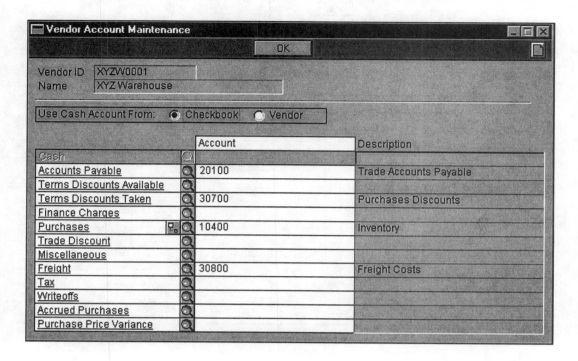

Account Maintenance Window — A/C #20210

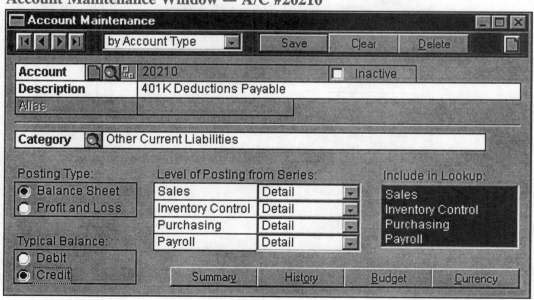

Employee Pay Code Maintenance - USA Window — Hourly Pay Code (HOUR)

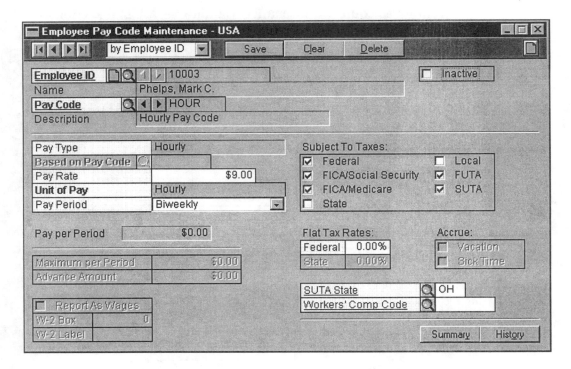

Employee Pay Code Maintenance - USA Window — Overtime Pay Code (OVER)

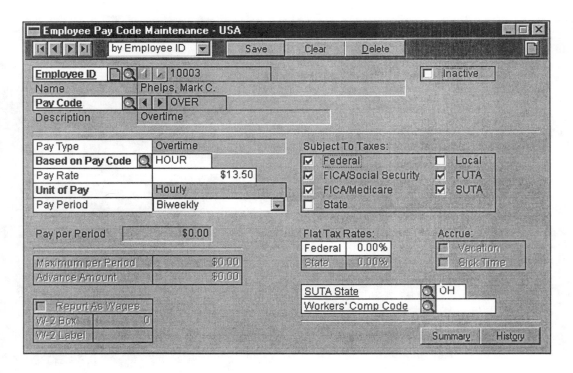

Item Maintenance Window — Item #103

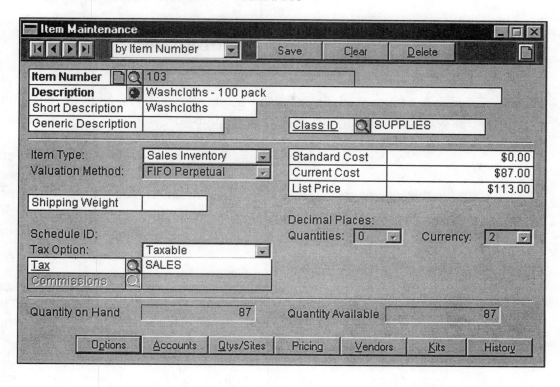

Chapter Summary

After completing Chapter 3, you should back up your data files for Jackson Supply Company using the instructions in Chapter 1.

You have now practiced the fifteen primary transactions and other activities listed on the first page of this chapter. You will use the knowledge you have gained in this chapter as you do Chapters 4 through 6. You are not, however, expected to be able to process transactions and do other activities without the use of the Reference book. You should plan to use the Reference book for all remaining parts of the project.

One way for you to summarize the information you have learned is to reread the brief Overview in the Reference book for each section. This Overview emphasizes what is being accomplished using *Dynamics*, not how to do the activity.

If you do not feel comfortable with your ability to complete each of the fifteen transactions and other activities listed on the first page of this chapter, you can practice further in one of two ways.

1.   You can do the entire chapter again by following the instructions in Chapter 1 to reinstall the *Dynamics* software. Doing so will return all data to its original form and permit you to practice all procedures again.

2.   You can do additional practice by completing any or most of the sections in this chapter again. You can continue to use Jackson Supply Co., since no subsequent chapters involve Jackson Supply Co. files.

Document numbers will, of course, be different if you redo sections without reinstalling the software. In addition, there are certain activities that you cannot do without first recording other information. For example, you cannot complete the Receive Goods on a Sales Return practice section without first recording the original sale in the Make a Credit Sale section. All practice sections that are dependent upon the completion of an earlier practice section are clearly identified in this chapter. Finally, you cannot do the bank reconciliation section again.

CHAPTER 4

Recording Transactions and Adjustments and Performing Month-end and Year-end Closing Procedures

Options A, B, and C. This chapter has three options depending upon your previous experience with a manual version systems project called the *Systems Understanding Aid,* written by the same authors as this computerized project. Option A is for students who have not used the *Systems Understanding Aid* before. Option B is for students who have completed the *Systems Understanding Aid* before. Option C is for students who have completed the *Systems Understanding Aid for Financial Accounting* before. Your Instructor will inform you which option or options you are to perform.

Option A

Introduction

In this chapter, you will record transactions for an existing company, Waren Distributing, Inc. for December 16-31, 1998. [Remember that date entry boxes in *Dynamics* default to your computer's current date. Thus, you will need to change them all back to 1998 dates for this project.] You will also complete other activities commonly done with accounting software and print several items to hand in to your instructor.

An important difference in this assignment compared to previous ones is the lack of detailed instructions for using *Dynamics* to record transactions and perform other activities.

If, at any time, you decide that you want to start the chapter over, you may do so by installing the *Dynamics* software again following Step 1 of the installation instructions in Chapter 1. You may want to do so if you have made errors that are too difficult to correct or if you believe that you do not understand the material in this chapter.

If you install the *Dynamics* software again, all previously installed *Dynamics* software and related data files are deleted. Assuming that you backed up the data files for Chapters 2 and 3 (Jackson Supply Co.), you can restore your data files for either or both chapters by following the instructions in Chapter 1.

In recording the transactions and performing the other activities for Waren Distributing, Inc., you will need four things:

1. **Information in this chapter**. The material instructs you what to record or do.
2. **Reference Summary Card**. Use this to locate the appropriate pages in the Reference book for recording transactions or doing other activities.
3. **Reference book**. Open the Reference book to the appropriate pages for the transaction you are recording or other activity you are doing and follow the instructions. In some cases, you will not have practiced using a Reference book section. You should not be concerned about this lack of practice.
4. *Dynamics* **software**.

Waren Distributing, Inc. is a wholesaler that sells small appliances. Waren's accountant has recorded all transactions for the year ended 12-31-98 through December 15, 1998 using *Dynamics*. For this assignment, you will do the following using *Dynamics*:

- Perform maintenance for inventory sales prices and costs.
- Record December 16 - 31 transactions and perform related maintenance.
- Perform December 1998 month-end procedures.
- Record 1998 year-end adjusting entries.
- Print financial statements and other reports.
- Perform year-end closing procedures.

Perform Maintenance for Inventory Sales Prices and Costs

The price and cost list on the next page reflects the current selling prices and costs for Waren's twelve products. Waren purchases all products for resale from one vendor, Super Electric Company. Waren sells each inventory item at the same price to all customers. A new price and cost list is prepared each time there is a change in an item's cost or selling price.

In this section, you will compare the selling price and cost of each product to the amounts included in *Dynamics* and update *Dynamics* for any differences.

Browse Button Hint

For efficiency in moving through the inventory items, you may use the browse buttons at the top left of the window. Use the browse button to the far left to move to the first record in a list. When finished with that record, use the browse button directly to the right of center to move to the next record in the list. If needed, the browse button directly to the left of center moves to the previous record in the list and the one on the far right moves to the last record in the list. These browse buttons are available in all windows involving multiple record files.

- *If you are not already working in Dynamics, open the Dynamics program.*
- *Open Waren Distributing, Inc.*
- *Perform maintenance for inventory sales prices and costs for each inventory item, following the guidance on page 123 of the Reference book. Be sure to save each inventory item changed before proceeding to the next inventory item.*

PRICE AND COST LIST
AS OF DECEMBER 15, 1998

Item No.	Description	Cost	Selling Price
AC-40	Alarm Clock	$15.00	$ 18.00
B-28	Blender	38.00	53.00
CM-15	Coffee Maker	39.00	60.00
CO-22	Can Opener	16.00	20.00
EFP-510	Electric Frying Pan	29.00	40.00
EK-48	Electric Knife	18.00	25.00
FP-2	Food Processor	90.00	135.00
HD-21	Hair Dryer	19.50	27.50
I-52	Iron	24.00	33.50
M-24	Mixer	25.50	35.00
SD-21	Smoke Detector	17.00	25.00
T-104	Toaster	27.00	40.00

After you complete inventory sales price and cost maintenance, the *Dynamics* files will contain the correct default sales price and cost for each inventory item. These sales prices and costs are used for all purchases and sales of inventory between December 16 and December 31, 1998.

Record December 16-31 Transactions and Perform Related Maintenance

The transactions on pages 4-7 to 4-12 for December 16 through December 31 should be dealt with in the order listed. Some of the transactions must be recorded whereas others require only maintenance.

In dealing with each transaction or maintenance task, the information you have already learned about *Dynamics* during Familiarization and Practice are used. You should use the Reference book and information from prior chapters to the extent you need it. Also, if you want to check whether information was recorded, it is easy to determine by using the Inquiry function.

Recall that most transaction entry windows in *Dynamics* provide access to an additional window for entering general ledger account distributions. All default general ledger distribution accounts are correct for Waren's December 16-31 transactions unless otherwise noted on pages 4-7 to 4-12.

The following is background information that you will need to record Waren's December 16-31 transactions.

Bank

Waren uses only one bank, First American Bank & Trust, for all deposits and checks, including payroll.

Credit Terms for Waren Distributing

Waren requires most of its customers to prepay for goods ordered. For these cash sales, the customer sends a check with its purchase order and Waren ships the merchandise. All trade discounts are already factored into the price list. Only a few favored customers with long-standing relationships with Waren and who buy larger quantities are granted credit. These favored customers receive the following cash discount for early payment: 2/10, Net 30.

Waren receives a similar cash discount from its main inventory supplier, Super Electric Company (2/10, Net 30). No cash discount is offered by Chicago Office Supply, whose invoices are payable upon receipt. All discount terms have already been included as default information in *Dynamics*.

Sales Tax for Waren Distributing

Waren Distributing makes only wholesale sales, which are exempt from state sales tax. Because Waren purchases all of its inventory for resale, there is also no sales tax on its inventory purchases. Sales tax of four percent applies to office supplies and fixed asset purchases. The correct sales tax percentages have already been included as default information in *Dynamics*.

Inventory Method

Waren uses the perpetual inventory method. All purchases of inventory are debited directly to the inventory account. Cost of goods sold for each sale is calculated automatically by *Dynamics*. Waren conducts a year-end physical inventory count and adjusts the perpetual inventory records as necessary. You will make those adjustments later.

WAREN DISTRIBUTING TRANSACTIONS FOR DECEMBER 16-31, 1998

Record each of the following transactions (#1-16) using Dynamics.

> • Hints are provided in boxed areas like this.

Use care in recording each transaction. **At a minimum, you should follow** *each step* **in the Quick Reference Table for each transaction**. It may take slightly more time, but it will almost certainly help you avoid serious errors. Find the appropriate Quick Reference Table for each transaction or other activity by using the Reference Summary Card.

Transaction#   December

1   16   **Prepare a purchase order:** Ordered the following inventory on account from Super Electric Co., Housewares Division, using purchase order No. 335. The goods will be received at the warehouse at a later date. The purchase order total is $20,600.

Units	Item #	Description
150	CO-22	Can opener
250	EFP-510	Electric frying pan
125	EK-48	Electric knife
250	HD-21	Hair dryer
150	M-24	Mixer

2   18   **Make a credit sale:** Received customer purchase order No. TX20901 in the mail from Fritter Appliance, approved their credit, prepared invoice No. 730 totaling $7,315, and shipped the goods from the warehouse. All goods ordered were shipped as follows:

Units	Item #	Description
30	AC-40	Alarm clock
50	CO-22	Can opener
25	FP-2	Food processor
60	T-104	Toaster

3   ·   **20**   **Change an employee record (employee maintenance):** Increased employee salary and wage rates, effective December 15. For hourly employees, overtime is paid at 1.5 times the regular hourly rate. There were no changes in filing status or withholding allowances.

Employee	New Salary/Wage Rate
Ray Kramer	$2,400, semimonthly
Jim Adams	$9.50 per hour
Nancy Ford	$8.40 per hour

- Select the Pay Codes button at the bottom of the Employee Maintenance-USA window to change pay rates.
- You will make a total of five pay rate changes for the three employees, including overtime pay rates: two each for the two hourly employees and one for the salaried employee. Save each pay rate change after entering it.
- When asked, "Do you want to roll down this rate change to all pay codes based on this pay code?", click "No".
- Remember to use the browse buttons to move through the employee records.

4   ⁵   **23**   **Write-off an uncollectible account receivable:** Received legal notification from Benson, Rosenbrook and Martinson, P.C., attorneys at law, that Okemos Housewares had filed bankruptcy and is unable to pay any of its outstanding debts to its suppliers. The $850 balance remaining on invoice #718 should therefore be written off as uncollectible. Waren uses the allowance method for recording bad debt expense.

5   ₹   **23**   **Collect an outstanding account receivable and make a bank deposit:** Received check No. 1643 for $2,500 from Bertram Appliance in partial payment of sales invoice No. 728, and deposited the check.

- After recording the cash receipt, record the deposit into the bank on the same day using the Bank Deposit Entry window (see pages 46-48 of the Reference book).

6   23   **Receive goods on a sales return:** Hanover Hardware returned 20 mixers and 20 alarm clocks that were originally purchased on invoice No. 729A. The goods are to be returned to "On Hand" status. Waren previously authorized Hanover Hardware by phone to return the goods for credit against their account balance. Hanover's return request #6256 was received with the goods. Sales return document CM 42 was issued for $1,060 and applied to invoice No. 729A.

- **Remember to apply sales return document CM 42 to invoice No. 729A** (*not* invoice No. 729). See steps R-X in the quick reference table.

---

7   23   **Collect an outstanding account receivable and make a bank deposit:** Received and deposited check No. 622 for $7,168.70 from Fritter Appliance for payment in full of invoice No. 730. The early payment discount taken by Fritter Appliance was $146.30.

- After recording the cash receipt, record the deposit into the bank on the same day using the Bank Deposit Entry window (see pages 46-48 of the Reference book).

---

8   24   **Receive goods from a purchase order:** Received merchandise from Super Electric as listed on purchase order No. 335, along with invoice #18719. The payment terms on the invoice are 2/10, Net 30. All merchandise listed on the purchase order was delivered in good condition and in the quantities ordered, except that only 100 hair dryers (Item No. HD 21) were received. The total of the invoice is $17,675. The goods were placed immediately in the inventory warehouse.

- Be sure to select "Shipment/Invoice," not "Shipment" in step B of the quick reference table.
- Be sure to do step G, click the Auto-Rcv button.
- You must enter account #10400, Inventory, as the Purchases account (Type = PURCH) in the Purchasing Distribution Entry window because the default account number will be blank.

---

9   ¿   24   **Purchase goods or services without a purchase order:** Received freight bill No. 78219 for $660 from Interstate Motor Freight and immediately issued check No. 257 for payment in full. The payment terms on the freight bill are Net 30.

> •   Be sure to enter the payment information for check No. 257. See step I in the quick reference table.

10   ℓ   24   **Make a cash sale and make a bank deposit:** Received and deposited check No. 5418 for $12,500 and customer purchase order No. 137592 in the mail from Redwood Fixtures for a cash sale. The goods were shipped from the warehouse and the cash sale was processed and recorded using invoice No. C-36. All goods ordered were shipped as follows:

Units	Item #	Description
50	CM-15	Coffee maker
100	EFP-510	Electric frying pans
200	HD-21	Hair dryers

> •   Do not forget steps N-S in the quick reference table (enter customer's payment information) or you will not be able to deposit the check.
> •   After recording the cash sale, record the deposit into the bank on the same day using the Bank Deposit Entry window (see pages 46-48 of the Reference book).

11   ◦   26   **Receive a miscellaneous cash receipt and make a bank deposit:** Borrowed and deposited $60,000 from First American Bank & Trust by issuing a two-year note payable. Check No. 545 for $60,000 was received and deposited.

> •   The credit portion of the transaction should be posted to account #21000, Notes Payable.
> •   After recording the cash receipt, record the deposit into the bank on the same day using the Bank Deposit Entry window (see pages 46-48 of the Reference book).

12   26   **Receive goods from a purchase order:** Received, and recorded as an expense, office supplies from Chicago Office Supply as listed on purchase order No. 334, which is shown as an open purchase order in *Dynamics*. Chicago Office Supply's vendor invoice No. 2294 was received with the goods, totaling $231.40 including sales tax. The payment terms on the invoice are "Upon receipt." All supplies ordered on purchase order No. 334 were received in good condition and taken to the warehouse.

> - Be sure to select "Shipment/Invoice", not "Shipment" in step B of the quick reference table.
> - You must enter account #40300, Office Supplies Expense, as the Purchases account (Type = PURCH) in the Purchasing Distribution Entry window because the default account number will be blank.

13   30   **Pay a vendor's outstanding invoice:** Issued check No. 258 for $17,321.50 to Super Electric for payment in full of invoice No. 18719 for goods received December 24. The early payment discount taken by Waren was $353.50.

14   31   **Pay employees:** Finished the payroll for the semimonthly pay period December 16-31, 1998, and issued checks No. 259-261 as follows:

Employee	Check#	Gross pay	Federal Tax Withheld	FICA Tax Withheld	Net pay
Ray Kramer	259	$2,400.00	$348.19	$192.00	$1,859.81
Jim Adams	260	$ 944.49	$ 94.95	$ 75.56	$ 773.98
Nancy Ford	261	$ 884.90	$ 47.11	$ 70.79	$ 767.00

15 . 31 **Receive goods from a purchase order:** Received a computer from Chicago Office Supply ordered on Waren's purchase order No. 332, which is shown as an open purchase order in *Dynamics*. Also received vendor's invoice No. 2305 from Chicago Office Supply, totaling $7,800 including sales tax. The payment terms on the invoice are "Upon receipt." The computer was received in new and undamaged condition in the warehouse. After it was unpacked and tested, it was taken directly to the office. It was not paid for.

- Be sure to select "Shipment/Invoice," not "Shipment," in step B of the quick reference table.
- Be sure to do step G, click the Auto-Rcv button.
- You must enter account #10800, Fixed Assets, *twice* in the Purchasing Distribution Entry window: once for the Purchases debit (Type = PURCH) and once for the Tax debit (Type = TAX). One of the default account numbers is blank and one is incorrect for a fixed asset purchase.

---

16 , 31 **Purchase goods or services without a purchase order:** Received vendor invoice No. 892 for $1,050 from the Chicago Daily Times for newspaper advertisements Waren ran during the Christmas season and immediately issued check No. 262 for payment in full. The payment terms on the invoice are "Upon receipt."

- Be sure to enter the payment information for check No. 262. See step I in the quick reference table.

Perform December 1998 Month-end Procedures

Because many of Waren's month-end procedures are done automatically by *Dynamics*, the only month-end procedures you will need to perform are:

- Accrue monthly unemployment taxes.
- Prepare the December bank reconciliation.
- Post December 16-31 transactions to the general ledger.
- Perform accounts receivable aging and print a customer monthly statement.

Prepare a General Journal Entry for Monthly Unemployment Taxes

Unemployment taxes for Waren's employees are imposed on the first $7,000 of wages paid during the year. The state unemployment rate (SUTA) is 2.7% and the Federal unemployment rate (FUTA) is 0.8%. As of December 1998, only one of Waren's employees, Nancy Ford, remains subject to unemployment taxes. Both SUTA and FUTA are accrued monthly through a general journal entry. The amounts for Nancy Ford for December are:

SUTA (account #20400)	$40.90
FUTA (account #20500)	12.12
Total (account #40600)	$53.02

⌨ *Record a general journal entry in Dynamics for the accrual of December's unemployment taxes.*

- Be sure that Account #40600 is the debit.

Prepare the December Bank Reconciliation

Check Figure for Your Cash Balance

Before starting the December bank reconciliation, be sure that your cash balance is correct by completing the following steps:

- 🖳 *Click Inquiry ➔ Financial ➔ Checkbook Register to open the Checkbook Register Inquiry window.*
- 🖳 *Select FIRST (First American Bank & Trust) in the Checkbook ID box.*

Review the contents of the Current Balance box. The balance should be $70,675.47. If it is not, the first thing to check is whether you remembered to record a bank deposit for transactions #5, 7, 10, and 11. If you forgot to record any or all bank deposits, record them now following the Reference book instructions on pages 46-48.

If you have recorded all bank deposits and your cash balance is still wrong in the Checkbook Register Inquiry window, return to the December 16-31 transactions to locate and correct any other errors before starting the bank reconciliation. When your cash balance is correct, continue with the requirements that follow.

Bank Reconciliation Information, Process, and Printing

As you process through the December reconciliation steps (computer symbols), do them in order and *do not click on the Reconcile button until told to do so*. You will need to print some reports first, and those reports will not be available after you click on the Reconcile button.

The following information is taken from the December bank statement and the November bank reconciliation, none of which is included in these materials:

- The December 31, 1998 bank statement balance is $34,294.26.

- The following checks have not cleared the bank as of December 31: checks #217, and #257 through #262.

- The December 26 deposit of loan proceeds has not cleared the bank as of December 31.

- A service charge of $28.50 is included on the December bank statement. *Note: The bank service charge should be posted to account #41000 — Other operating expense.*

🖥 *Prepare the December bank reconciliation,* **but do not click the Reconcile button** *yet (step R in the quick reference table on page 92 of the Reference book) because you need to print the reconciliation first.* The cutoff date for the bank reconciliation is December 31, 1998.

🖥 *When the reconciliation is correct, click File → Print to open the Print Reconciliation Reports window.*

🖥 *Remove the check marks next to the following reports so that they do not print: Bank Adjustments Edit List and Marked Transactions Report. Then click the OK button.* A Report Destination window will open for the first checked report, Reconciliation Edit List.

🖥 *Select Screen as the output destination and click OK.* Next you will get the Report Destination window for the Outstanding Transactions Report.

🖥 *Select Screen again and click OK.* This will bring up the screen output for the first report selected, Reconcile Journal.

🖥 *Click the print button in the top left corner of this window to print the reconciliation. Click OK at the next window asking about number of copies.*

🖥 *Repeat the previous step for the next output screen to come up, Outstanding Transactions Report.*

🖥 *Review your printed output for accuracy and acceptability.* These reports will be handed in to your instructor along with year-end reports.

🖥 *Click the Reconcile button in the Select Bank Transactions window (step R in the quick reference table on page 92 of the Reference book).*

Post December 16 - 31 Transactions to the General Ledger

Waren's accountant posted all transactions to the general ledger through December 15, 1998. You are to post the December 16-31 transactions to the general ledger.

🖥 *Post the December 16-31 transactions using the instructions in the Reference book on pages 124-127.* Although you have not practiced posting, it is easy to do when following the Reference book.

Age Accounts Receivable and
Print Customer Monthly Statements

Before customer monthly statements can be prepared, you must perform the *Dynamics* aging routine for accounts receivable. Before you do so, read the Age Accounts Receivable and Print Customer Monthly Statements Overview on page 128 of the Reference book.

💻 *Complete the accounts receivable aging process as of 12-31-98 for Waren, (steps A-E in the quick reference table on page 128).*

At the end of each month, Waren sends monthly statements to all customers with an outstanding balance. For this section, you are to print a hard copy of the December monthly statement for Bertram Appliance.

💻 *Print a hard copy of the December monthly statement for Bertram Appliance, using the Reference book instructions on pages 131-132 (steps F-N in the quick reference table on page 128).*

Print a General Ledger Trial Balance for
Check Figures Prior to Year-End Adjusting Entries

The trial balance on page 4-22 shows the correct balances in all general ledger accounts after the December month-end procedures are completed.

💻 *Select a general ledger trial balance (quick summary) for Waren and print a hard copy of the 12-31-98 balances using the Reference book instructions on pages 134-139 and the Select Reports section of the Reference Summary Card. Note: Due to a small font size, you cannot view the trial balance numbers on the screen before printing.*

Compare the amounts on your printed trial balance with those on page 4-22. If any amounts are different, return to the December 16-31 transactions and the month-end procedures you processed in *Dynamics* and make the necessary corrections. See Appendix A in the Reference book for error correction instructions. When all errors are corrected, print a corrected trial balance.

When your balances agree with those on page 4-22, go to the next section where you will record year-end adjusting entries.

Adjust Perpetual Inventory Records and Prepare General Journal Entries for the 1998 Year-end

The next step at the end of an accounting year before printing output is to record year-end adjusting entries. The following are the types of adjusting entries you will make:

- Physical inventory adjustment
- Depreciation expense
- Accrued interest payable
- Bad debt expense and allowance
- Cost of goods sold
- Federal income taxes

Each of the adjusting entries is explained in a section that follows. Make the adjustments in the order listed.

Adjust Perpetual Inventory Records and Post Transactions to the General Ledger

The physical count taken on December 31 indicated that there were disagreements between the physical count and the perpetual records for certain items. Management is concerned about these inventory differences, but knows that the physical count is accurate. Thus, the current perpetual records must be adjusted as follows to agree with the physical count:

Item No.	Description	Quantity on Perpetual Records	Quantity per Physical Count
B-28	Blender	92	98
FP-2	Food processor	127	124
T-104	Toaster	247	236

⌨ *Record the inventory adjustments in Dynamics.*

⌨ *After recording the inventory adjustment, post the transaction to the general ledger (pages 124-127 of the Reference book).* Note: This step is not necessary for the remaining year-end adjusting entries because they are all prepared using the Transaction Entry window, which posts directly to the general ledger.

After the inventory adjustment is posted, you should record the remaining five year-end adjusting entries.

Record each of the remaining five year-end adjusting entries by preparing a general journal entry in Dynamics using the information provided in the next five sections.

Depreciation Expense

Depreciation expense is calculated once annually at the end of each year and recorded in the general journal as of December 31. Total depreciation expense for 1998 is $16,256.80. General ledger account numbers for the *Dynamics* journal entry are: #40400 (Depreciation expense) and #10900 (Accumulated depreciation).

Accrued Interest Payable

Recall from transaction #11 on page 4-10 that Waren has a $60,000 two-year note payable to First American Bank & Trust dated December 26, 1998. The stated annual interest rate on the note is 10%. The terms of the note payable call for the following payments:

- $6,000 interest payments on 12-26-99 and 12-26-00
- $60,000 principal payment on 12-26-00

Interest accruals are calculated using a 365-day year with the day the note was made counting as the first day. General ledger account numbers for the journal entry are: #40800 (Interest expense) and #20900 (Interest payable).

Bad Debt Expense and Allowance

Bad debt expense is estimated once annually at the end of each year as 1/4 of one percent of net sales and is recorded in the general journal as of December 31. The "allowance" method of recording bad debt expense is used. General ledger account numbers for the journal entry are: #40900 (Bad debt expense) and #10300 (Allowance for doubtful accounts).

- Use the Reports function in *Dynamics* to determine annual net sales from the income statement. **Be sure to change the current date on your computer (top right corner of the screen) to 12/31/98 before opening the report window**.

659,289.50

Cost of Goods Sold

Dynamics automatically debits cost of goods sold and credits inventory for the product cost for each sale. Waren treats purchase discounts taken and freight-in as a part of cost of goods sold, but records them in separate accounts during the accounting period. Therefore, these two accounts must be closed to cost of goods sold (account #30400): purchases discounts taken (#30700) and freight-in (#30800).

(8397.85)   9171.00

- Before preparing the general journal entry, use the Inquiry function in *Dynamics* to determine the balance in each account being closed to cost of goods sold (*Inquiry → Financial → Summary*, then review the contents of the Total box for each account to be closed).

93354.58
13252.32
181443.35

7500
6250

Federal Income Taxes

Assume that corporate income tax rates for 1998 are: 15% of the first $50,000 of income, plus 25% of the next $25,000, plus 36% of all income over $75,000. General ledger account numbers for the journal entry are: #40700 (Federal income tax expense) and #20700 (Federal income taxes payable).

- After all other adjusting entries are recorded, use the Reports function in *Dynamics* to determine pre-tax income from the income statement for the calculation of federal income tax expense. **Be sure the current date on your computer is 12/31/98 before opening the report window.**

Print a General Ledger Trial Balance for
Check Figures After Year-End Adjusting Entries

The trial balance on pages 4-23 and 4-24 shows the correct balances in all general ledger accounts after the year-end adjusting entries are recorded.

⌨ *Select a general ledger trial balance (quick summary) for Waren and print a hard copy of the 12-31-98 balances.* This report will be handed in to your instructor along with year-end reports.

Compare the balances on your printed trial balance with those on pages 4-23 and 4-24. If the amounts on your printed trial balance are different, return to the year-end adjusting entries and make the necessary corrections before printing a corrected trial balance. See Appendix A in the Reference book for error correction instructions. When your balances agree with those on pages 4-23 and 4-24, go to the next section where you will print output.

Print Financial Statements and Other Reports

All entries have now been recorded.

🖳 *Print the following standard reports using the Reference Summary Card.* **For the two financial statements, be sure the current date is 12/31/98 before requesting the report.**

- Balance sheet
- Statement of income and retained earnings
- General journal (cross-reference report by journal entry) for December
- Account receivable aged trial balance
- Accounts payable aged trial balance
- Inventory stock status report as of 12-31-98
- Employee earnings register for 1998

🖳 *Print the following custom reports for December, following the instructions on pages 140-144 of the Reference book.*

- Sales listing
- Cash receipts listing
- Purchases listing
- Check listing
- Payroll listing

Hand in all reports to your course instructor, including the bank reconciliation reports, the customer monthly statement for Bertram Appliance, and the quick summary trial balance after year-end adjustments that you printed in previous sections.

Perform Year-end Closing Procedures

After all reports are printed, the next step is to close the general ledger for the current year. The closing process in *Dynamics* closes all income statement accounts to the retained earnings account and sets up the new fiscal year for Waren.

After all output is printed and determined to be satisfactory, complete the year-end closing procedures described in the Reference book on pages 146-149. Keep in mind that once you perform closing procedures, you can make corrections only to balance sheet accounts.

All procedures are now complete for this chapter. Now that you have completed Chapter 4, you should back up your data file for Waren Distributing, Inc. following the instructions in Chapter 1.

Account	Description	Beginning Balance	Net Change	Ending Balance
10100	Cash	$9,832.17	$60,814.80	$70,646.97
10200	Accounts Receivable	$14,724.00	($2,470.00)	$12,254.00
10300	Allowance for Doubtful Accounts	($1,536.25)	$1,936.25	$400.00
10400	Inventory	$41,325.00	$19,989.00	$61,314.00
10600	Marketable Securities	$0.00	$8,000.00	$8,000.00
10800	Fixed Assets	$128,490.00	$16,068.00	$144,558.00
10900	Accumulated Depreciation	($17,017.00)	$0.00	($17,017.00)
20100	Accounts Payable	($17,398.50)	$9,367.10	($8,031.40)
20300	Federal Income Taxes Withheld	($517.82)	($368.88)	($886.70)
20400	State Unemployment Taxes Payable	($68.90)	$28.00	($40.90)
20500	Federal Unemployment Taxes Payable	($17.15)	$5.03	($12.12)
20600	F.I.C.A. Taxes Payable	($415.00)	($852.20)	($1,267.20)
20700	Federal Income Taxes Payable	($3,187.00)	$3,187.00	$0.00
21000	Notes Payable	$0.00	($60,000.00)	($60,000.00)
26000	Common Stock	($75,000.00)	$0.00	($75,000.00)
29000	Retained Earnings	($79,213.55)	$0.00	($79,213.55)
30100	Sales	$0.00	($659,289.50)	($659,289.50)
30200	Sales Returns and Allowances	$0.00	$32,070.00	$32,070.00
30300	Sales Discounts Taken	$0.00	$4,855.63	$4,855.63
30400	Cost of Goods Sold	$0.00	$440,014.00	$440,014.00
30700	Purchases Discounts Taken	$0.00	($8,397.85)	($8,397.85)
30800	Freight-in	$0.00	$9,171.00	$9,171.00
31200	Miscellaneous Revenue	$0.00	($275.00)	($275.00)
40100	Rent Expense	$0.00	$19,200.00	$19,200.00
40200	Advertising Expense	$0.00	$7,848.00	$7,848.00
40300	Office Supplies Expense	$0.00	$4,333.68	$4,333.68
40500	Wages and Salaries Expense	$0.00	$77,822.36	$77,822.36
40600	Payroll Tax Expense	$0.00	$6,839.08	$6,839.08
41000	Other Operating Expense	$0.00	$10,104.50	$10,104.50

Total Accounts: 29

Grand Totals: $0.00 $0.00 $0.00

Waren Distributing, Inc.
QUICK TRIAL BALANCE SUMMARY FOR 1998
General Ledger

Account	Description	Beginning Balance	Net Change	Ending Balance
10100	Cash	$9,832.17	$60,814.80	$70,646.97
10200	Accounts Receivable	$14,724.00	($2,470.00)	$12,254.00
10300	Allowance for Doubtful Accounts	($1,536.25)	$380.34	($1,155.91)
10400	Inventory	$41,325.00	$19,650.00	$60,975.00
10600	Marketable Securities	$0.00	$8,000.00	$8,000.00
10800	Fixed Assets	$128,490.00	$16,068.00	$144,558.00
10900	Accumulated Depreciation	($17,017.00)	($16,256.80)	($33,273.80)
20100	Accounts Payable	($17,398.50)	$9,367.10	($8,031.40)
20300	Federal Income Taxes Withheld	($517.82)	($368.88)	($886.70)
20400	State Unemployment Taxes Payable	($68.90)	$28.00	($40.90)
20500	Federal Unemployment Taxes Payable	($17.15)	$5.03	($12.12)
20600	F.I.C.A. Taxes Payable	($415.00)	($852.20)	($1,267.20)
20700	Federal Income Taxes Payable	($3,187.00)	($2,431.06)	($5,618.06)
20900	Interest Payable	$0.00	($98.63)	($98.63)
21000	Notes Payable	$0.00	($60,000.00)	($60,000.00)
26000	Common Stock	($75,000.00)	$0.00	($75,000.00)
29000	Retained Earnings	($79,213.55)	$0.00	($79,213.55)
30100	Sales	$0.00	($659,289.50)	($659,289.50)
30200	Sales Returns and Allowances	$0.00	$32,070.00	$32,070.00
30300	Sales Discounts Taken	$0.00	$4,855.63	$4,855.63
30400	Cost of Goods Sold	$0.00	$441,126.15	$441,126.15
30700	Purchases Discounts Taken	$0.00	$0.00	$0.00
30800	Freight-in	$0.00	$0.00	$0.00
31200	Miscellaneous Revenue	$0.00	($275.00)	($275.00)
40100	Rent Expense	$0.00	$19,200.00	$19,200.00
40200	Advertising Expense	$0.00	$7,848.00	$7,848.00
40300	Office Supplies Expense	$0.00	$4,333.68	$4,333.68
40400	Depreciation Expense	$0.00	$16,256.80	$16,256.80
40500	Wages and Salaries Expense	$0.00	$77,822.36	$77,822.36
40600	Payroll Tax Expense	$0.00	$6,839.08	$6,839.08

Account   Description

		Beginning Balance	Net Change	Ending Balance

40700	Federal Income Tax Expense			
		$0.00	$5,618.06	$5,618.06
40800	Interest Expense			
		$0.00	$98.63	$98.63
40900	Bad Debt Expense			
		$0.00	$1,555.91	$1,555.91
41000	Other Operating Expense			
		$0.00	$10,104.50	$10,104.50

Total Accounts: 34

    Grand Totals: $0.00 $0.00 $0.00

Option B

Introduction

In this chapter, you will record the same December 16-31, 1998 transactions for Waren Distributing, Inc. that you did in the *Systems Understanding Aid (SUA)*. [Remember that date entry boxes in *Dynamics* default to your computer's current date. Thus, you will need to change them all back to 1998 dates for this project.] You will also complete other activities commonly done with accounting software and print several items to hand in to your instructor.

An important difference in this assignment compared to previous ones is the lack of detailed instructions for using *Dynamics* to record transactions and perform other activities.

If, at any time, you decide that you want to start the chapter over, you may do so by installing the *Dynamics* software again following Step 1 of the installation instructions in Chapter 1. You may want to do so if you have made errors that are too difficult to correct or if you believe that you do not understand the material in this chapter.

If you install the *Dynamics* software again, all previously installed *Dynamics* software and related data files are deleted. Assuming that you backed up the data files for Chapters 2 and 3 (Jackson Supply Co.), you can restore your data files for either or both chapters by following the instructions in Chapter 1.

In recording the transactions and performing the other activities for Waren Distributing, Inc., you will need several things:

- **Optional Items from the *SUA*** (not required; all necessary information from the *SUA* has been incorporated in this chapter):
  - Instructions, Flowcharts and Ledgers book
  - Journals book
  - All year-end financial statements and schedules you prepared for Waren Distributing in the *SUA*
- **Information in this chapter**. The material instructs you what to record or do.
- **Reference Summary Card**. Use this to locate the appropriate pages in the Reference book for recording transactions or doing other activities.

- **Reference book**. Open the Reference book to the appropriate pages for the transaction you are recording or other activity you are doing and follow the instructions. In some cases, you will not have practiced using a Reference book section. You should not be concerned about this lack of practice.
- *Dynamics* **software**.

Jim Adams has recorded all transactions for the year ended 12-31-98 through December 15, 1998 using *Dynamics*. This is consistent with the *SUA*. For this assignment, you will do the following using *Dynamics*:

- Perform maintenance for inventory sales prices and costs.
- Record December 16 - 31 transactions and perform related maintenance.
- Perform December, 1998 month-end procedures.
- Record 1998 year-end adjusting entries.
- Print financial statements and other reports.
- Perform year-end closing procedures.

When you are finished, the financial statements and other results will be the same as the correct solution for the *Systems Understanding Aid*.

Perform Maintenance for Inventory Sales Prices and Costs

The price and cost list on the next page, taken from the *SUA*, reflects the current selling prices and costs for Waren's twelve products. In this section, you will compare the selling price and cost of each product to the amounts included in *Dynamics* and update *Dynamics* for any differences.

Browse Button Hint

For efficiency in moving through the inventory items, you may use the browse buttons at the top left of the window. Use the browse button to the far left to move to the first record in a list. When finished with that record, use the browse button directly to the right of center to move to the next record in the list. If needed, the browse button directly to the left of center moves to the previous record in the list and the one on the far right moves to the last record in the list. These browse buttons are available in all windows involving multiple record files.

- 💻 *If you are not already working in Dynamics, open the Dynamics program.*
- 💻 *Open Waren Distributing, Inc.*
- 💻 *Perform maintenance for inventory sales prices and costs for each inventory item, following the guidance on page 123 of the Reference book.* Be sure to save each inventory item changed before proceeding to the next inventory item.

**PRICE AND COST LIST
AS OF DECEMBER 15, 1998**

Item No.	Description	Cost	Selling Price
AC-40	Alarm Clock	$15.00	$ 18.00
B-28	Blender	38.00	53.00
CM-15	Coffee Maker	39.00	60.00
CO-22	Can Opener	16.00	20.00
EFP-510	Electric Frying Pan	29.00	40.00
EK-48	Electric Knife	18.00	25.00
FP-2	Food Processor	90.00	135.00
HD-21	Hair Dryer	19.50	27.50
I-52	Iron	24.00	33.50
M-24	Mixer	25.50	35.00
SD-21	Smoke Detector	17.00	25.00
T-104	Toaster	27.00	40.00

After you complete inventory sales price and cost maintenance, the *Dynamics* files will contain the correct default sales price and cost for each inventory item. These sales prices and costs are used for all purchases and sales of inventory between December 16 and December 31, 1998.

Record December 16-31 Transactions and Perform Related Maintenance

The transactions on pages 4-28 to 4-34 for December 16 through December 31 are the same as the transactions you recorded in the *SUA*, except where noted. Events and information that are not necessary to process the transactions in *Dynamics* have been removed. In addition, supplemental information from the *SUA* documents has been incorporated into the *Dynamics* transactions list so that you will not need the *SUA* transactions list or the *SUA* documents to complete this section. The transactions should be dealt with in the order listed. Some of the transactions must be recorded whereas others require only maintenance.

In dealing with each transaction or maintenance task, the information you have already learned about *Dynamics* during Familiarization and Practice are used. You should use the *Dynamics* Reference book and information from prior chapters to the extent you need it. Also, if you want to check whether information was recorded, it is easy to determine by using the Inquiry function. You can also compare each transaction you record in *Dynamics* to the result you obtained when you did the *SUA*, although this is not required. Use the *SUA* journals book for this comparison.

Recall that most transaction entry windows in *Dynamics* provide access to an additional window for entering general ledger account distributions. All default general ledger distribution accounts are correct for Waren's December 16-31 transactions unless otherwise noted on pages 4-28 to 4-34.

WAREN DISTRIBUTING TRANSACTIONS FOR DECEMBER 16-31, 1998

⌨ *Record each of the following transactions (#1-16) using Dynamics.*

●   Hints are provided in boxed areas like this.

Use care in recording each transaction. **At a minimum, you should follow** *each step* **in the Quick Reference Table for each transaction**. It may take slightly more time, but it will almost certainly help you avoid serious errors. Find the appropriate Quick Reference Table for each transaction or other activity by using the Reference Summary Card.

Transaction#   December

1   16   **Prepare a purchase order:** Ordered the following inventory on account from Super Electric Co., Housewares Division, using purchase order No. 335. The goods will be received at the warehouse at a later date. The purchase order total is $20,600.

Units	Item #	Description
150	CO-22	Can opener
250	EFP-510	Electric frying pan
125	EK-48	Electric knife
250	HD-21	Hair dryer
150	M-24	Mixer

2   **18**   **Make a credit sale:** Received customer purchase order No. TX20901 in the mail from Fritter Appliance, approved their credit, prepared invoice No. 730, totaling $7,315, and shipped the goods from the warehouse. All goods ordered were shipped as follows:

Units	Item #	Description
30	AC-40	Alarm clock
50	CO-22	Can opener
25	FP-2	Food processor
60	T-104	Toaster

3   **20**   **Change an employee record (employee maintenance):** Increased employee salary and wage rates, effective December 15. Recall that for hourly employees, overtime is paid at 1.5 times the regular hourly rate. There were no changes in filing status or withholding allowances. *Note: Ignore the federal income tax withholding amount changes in the SUA.*

Employee	New Salary/Wage Rate
Ray Kramer	$2,400, semimonthly
Jim Adams	$9.50 per hour
Nancy Ford	$8.40 per hour

- Select the Pay Codes button at the bottom of the Employee Maintenance-USA window to change pay rates.
- You will make a total of five pay rate changes for the three employees, including overtime pay rates: two each for the two hourly employees and one for the salaried employee. Save each pay rate change after entering it.
- When asked, "Do you want to roll down this rate change to all pay codes based on this pay code?", click "No."
- Remember to use the browse buttons to move through the employee records.

4   **23**   **Write-off an uncollectible account receivable:** Received legal notification from Benson, Rosenbrook and Martinson, P.C., attorneys at law, that Okemos Housewares had filed bankruptcy and is unable to pay any of its outstanding debts to its suppliers. The $850 balance remaining on invoice #718 should therefore be written off as uncollectible. Recall that Waren uses the allowance method for recording bad debt expense.

5   23   **Collect an outstanding account receivable and make a bank deposit:** Received check No. 1643 for $2,500 from Bertram Appliance in partial payment of sales invoice No. 728, and deposited the check.

> ● After recording the cash receipt, record the deposit into the bank on the same day using the Bank Deposit Entry window (see pages 46-48 of the Reference book).

6   23   **Receive goods on a sales return:** Hanover Hardware returned 20 mixers and 20 alarm clocks that were originally purchased on invoice No. 729A. The goods are to be returned to "On Hand" status. Waren previously authorized Hanover Hardware by phone to return the goods for credit against their account balance. Hanover's return request No. 6256 was received with the goods. Sales return document CM 42 was issued for $1,060 and applied to invoice No. 729A.

Note: Invoice No. 729 from the SUA was split into two transactions in Dynamics: invoice Nos. 729 and 729A. This was done to simplify the use of Dynamics.

> ● **Remember to apply sales return document CM 42 to invoice No. 729A** (*not* invoice No. 729). See steps R-X in the quick reference table.

7   23   **Collect an outstanding account receivable and make a bank deposit:** Received and deposited check No. 6401 for $642.88 from Hanover Hardware for payment in full of invoice No. 729. The early payment discount taken by Hanover was $13.12.

> ● Remember to apply the cash receipt to invoice No. 729, *not* No. 729A.
> ● After recording the cash receipt, record the deposit into the bank on the same day using the Bank Deposit Entry window (see pages 46-48 of the Reference book).

8	24	**Receive goods from a purchase order:** Received merchandise from Super Electric as listed on purchase order No. 335, along with invoice #18719 totaling $17,675. The payment terms on the invoice are 2/10, Net 30. All merchandise listed on the purchase order was delivered in good condition and in the quantities ordered, except that only 100 hair dryers (Item No. HD 21) were received. The goods were placed immediately in the inventory warehouse.

- Be sure to select "Shipment/Invoice," not "Shipment" in step B of the quick reference table.
- Be sure to do step G, click the Auto-Rcv button.
- You must enter account #10400, Inventory, as the Purchases account (Type = PURCH) in the Purchasing Distribution Entry window because the default account number will be blank.

9	24	**Purchase goods or services without a purchase order:** Received freight bill No. 78219 for $660 from Interstate Motor Freight and immediately issued check No. 257 for payment in full. The freight bill relates to the merchandise received from purchase order No. 335. The payment terms on the freight bill are Net 30.

- Be sure to enter the payment information for check No. 257. See step I in the quick reference table.

10	24	**Make a cash sale and make a bank deposit:** Received and deposited check No. 5418 for $12,500 and customer purchase order No. 137592 in the mail from Redwood Fixtures for a cash sale. The goods were shipped from the warehouse and the cash sale was processed and recorded using invoice No. C-36. All goods ordered were shipped as follows:

Units	Item #	Description
50	CM-15	Coffee maker
100	EFP-510	Electric frying pans
200	HD-21	Hair dryers

- Do not forget steps N-S in the quick reference table (enter customer's payment information) or you will not be able to deposit the check.
- After recording the cash sale, record the deposit into the bank on the same day using the Bank Deposit Entry window (see pages 46-48 of the Reference book).

| 11 | 26 | **Receive a miscellaneous cash receipt and make a bank deposit:** Borrowed and deposited $60,000 from First American Bank & Trust by issuing a two-year note payable. Check No. 545 for $60,000 was received and deposited. |

- The credit portion of the transaction should be posted to account #21000, Notes Payable.
- After recording the cash receipt, record the deposit into the bank on the same day using the Bank Deposit Entry window (see pages 46-48 of the Reference book).

| 12 | 26 | **Receive goods from a purchase order:** Received, and recorded as an expense, office supplies from Chicago Office Supply as listed on purchase order No. 334, which is shown as an open purchase order in *Dynamics*. Chicago Office Supply's vendor invoice No. 2294 was received with the goods, totaling $231.40 including sales tax. The payment terms on the invoice are "Upon receipt." All supplies ordered on purchase order No. 334 were received in good condition and taken directly to the warehouse. |

- Be sure to select "Shipment/Invoice," not "Shipment" in step B of the quick reference table.
- You must enter account #40300, Office Supplies Expense, as the Purchases account (Type = PURCH) in the Purchasing Distribution Entry window because the default account number will be blank.

| 13 | 30 | **Pay a vendor's outstanding invoice:** Issued check No. 258 for $17,321.50 to Super Electric for payment in full of invoice No. 18719 for goods received December 24. The early payment discount taken by Waren was $353.50. |

14   31   **Pay employees:** Finished the payroll for the semimonthly pay period December 16-31, 1998, and issued checks No. 259-261 as follows:

Employee	Check#	Gross pay	Federal Tax Withheld	FICA Tax Withheld	Net pay
Ray Kramer	259	$2,400.00	$348.19	$192.00	$1,859.81
Jim Adams	260	$ 944.49	$ 94.95	$ 75.56	$ 773.98
Nancy Ford	261	$ 884.90	$ 47.11	$ 70.79	$ 767.00

- For Nancy Ford and Jim Adams (hourly employees), ignore the distinction between regular and overtime hours and earnings from the *SUA* when recording the payroll checks in *Dynamics*. Regular and overtime earnings are reflected in the Gross pay amounts shown above, and both should be entered under the HOUR pay code in the Payroll Manual Check Transaction Entry - USA window.

15   31   **Receive goods from a purchase order:** Received a computer from Chicago Office Supply ordered on Waren's purchase order No. 332, which is shown as an open purchase order in *Dynamics*. Also received vendor's invoice No. 2305 from Chicago Office Supply, totaling $7,800 including sales tax. The payment terms on the invoice are "Upon receipt". The computer was received in new and undamaged condition in the warehouse. After it was unpacked and tested, it was taken directly to the office. It was not paid for.

- Be sure to select "Shipment/Invoice," not "Shipment," in step B of the quick reference table.
- Be sure to do step G, click the Auto-Rcv button.
- You must enter account #10800, Fixed Assets, *twice* in the Purchasing Distribution Entry window: once for the Purchases debit (Type = PURCH) and once for the Tax debit (Type = TAX). One of the default account numbers is blank and one is incorrect for a fixed asset purchase.

16   31   **Purchase goods or services without a purchase order:** Received vendor invoice No. 892 for $1,050 from the Chicago Daily Times for newspaper advertisements Waren ran during the Christmas season and immediately issued check No. 262 for payment in full. The payment terms on the invoice are "Upon receipt."

- Be sure to enter the payment information for check No. 262. See step I in the quick reference table.

Perform December 1998 Month-end Procedures

Because many of Waren's month-end procedures are done automatically by *Dynamics*, the only month-end procedures you will need to perform are:

- Accrue monthly unemployment taxes.
- Prepare the December bank reconciliation.
- Post December 16-31 transactions to the general ledger.
- Perform accounts receivable aging and print a customer monthly statement.

Prepare a General Journal Entry for
Monthly Unemployment Taxes

Recall from the *SUA* that only one of Waren's employees, Nancy Ford, remains subject to federal and state unemployment taxes as of December, 1998. The amounts for Nancy Ford for December are:

SUTA (account #20400)	$40.90
FUTA (account #20500)	12.12
Total (account #40600)	$53.02

Note that all information necessary for the journal entry is also included in the *SUA* general journal. *Note: Ignore the employer's F.I.C.A. portion of the entry in the SUA general journal; Dynamics automatically calculates this amount for each pay check.*

Record a general journal entry in Dynamics for the accrual of December's federal and state unemployment taxes.

- Be sure that Account #40600 is the debit.

Prepare the December Bank Reconciliation

Check Figure for Your Cash Balance

Before starting the December bank reconciliation, be sure that your cash balance is correct by completing the following steps:

🖥 *Click Inquiry → Financial → Checkbook Register to open the Checkbook Register Inquiry window.*

🖥 *Select FIRST (First American Bank & Trust) in the Checkbook ID box.*

Review the contents of the Current Balance box. The balance should be $64,149.65. If it is not, the first thing to check is whether you remembered to record a bank deposit for transactions #5, 7, 10, and 11. If you forgot to record any or all bank deposits, record them now following the Reference book instructions on pages 46-48.

If you have recorded all bank deposits and your cash balance is still wrong in the Checkbook Register Inquiry window, return to the December 16-31 transactions to locate and correct any other errors before starting the bank reconciliation. When your cash balance is correct, continue with the requirements that follow.

Bank Reconciliation Information, Process, and Printing

As you process through the December reconciliation steps (computer symbols), do them in order and *do not click on the Reconcile button until told to do so*. You will need to print some reports first, and those reports will not be available after you click on the Reconcile button.

The following information is taken from the December bank statement and the November bank reconciliation, none of which is included in these materials:

- The December 31, 1998 bank statement balance is $27,768.44.

- The following checks have not cleared the bank as of December 31: checks #217, and #257 through #262.

- The December 26 deposit of loan proceeds has not cleared the bank as of December 31.

- A service charge of $28.50 is included on the December bank statement. *Note: The bank service charge should be posted to account #41000 — Other operating expense.*

- *Prepare the December bank reconciliation, **but do not click the Reconcile button yet** (step R in the quick reference table on page 92 of the Reference book) because you need to print the reconciliation first.* The cutoff date for the bank reconciliation is December 31, 1998.

- *When the reconciliation is correct, click File → Print to open the Print Reconciliation Reports window.*

- *Remove the check marks next to the following reports so that they do not print: Bank Adjustments Edit List and Marked Transactions Report. Then click the OK button.* A Report Destination window will open for the first checked report, Reconciliation Edit List.

- *Select Screen as the output destination and click OK.* Next you will get the Report Destination window for the Outstanding Transactions Report.

- *Select Screen again and click OK.* This will bring up the screen output for the first report selected, Reconcile Journal.

- *Click the print button in the top left corner of this window to print the reconciliation. Click OK at the next window asking about number of copies.*

- *Repeat the previous step for the next output screen to come up, Outstanding Transactions Report.*

- *Review your printed output for accuracy and acceptability.* These reports will be handed in to your instructor along with year-end reports.

- *Click the Reconcile button in the Select Bank Transactions window (step R in the quick reference table on page 92 of the Reference book).*

Post December 16 - 31 Transactions to the General Ledger

Waren's accountant posted all transactions to the general ledger through December 15, 1998. You are to post the December 16-31 transactions to the general ledger.

- *Post the December 16-31 transactions using the instructions in the Reference book on pages 124-127.* Although you have not practiced posting, it is easy to do when following the Reference book.

Age Accounts Receivable and
Print Customer Monthly Statements

Before customer monthly statements can be prepared, you must perform the *Dynamics* aging routine for accounts receivable. Before you do so, read the Age Accounts Receivable and Print Customer Monthly Statements Overview on page 128 of the Reference book.

Complete the accounts receivable aging process as of 12-31-98 for Waren, (steps A-E in the quick reference table on page 128).

At the end of each month, Waren sends monthly statements to all customers with an outstanding balance. For this section, you are to print a hard copy of the December monthly statement for Bertram Appliance.

Print a hard copy of the December monthly statement for Bertram Appliance, using the Reference book instructions on pages 131-132 (steps F-N in the quick reference table on page 128).

Print a General Ledger Trial Balance for
Check Figures Prior to Year-End Adjusting Entries

The trial balance on page 4-44 shows the correct balances in all general ledger accounts after the December month-end procedures are completed.

Select a general ledger trial balance (quick summary) for Waren and print a hard copy of the 12-31-98 balances using the Reference book instructions on pages 134-139 and the Select Reports section of the Reference Summary Card. Note: Due to a small font size, you cannot view the trial balance numbers on the screen before printing.

Compare the amounts on your printed trial balance with those on page 4-44. If any amounts are different, return to the December 16-31 transactions and the month-end procedures you processed in *Dynamics* and make the necessary corrections. See Appendix A in the Reference book for error correction instructions. When all errors are corrected, print a corrected trial balance.

You can also compare the amounts on your printed trial balance with those included in the *SUA* year-end unadjusted trial balance (part of the year-end worksheet). All account balances should agree if your solution to the *SUA* was correct except inventory-related accounts. Inventory-related account balances do not agree because of the use of different inventory methods. The balances will agree after adjusting entries are completed. See pages 4-38 to 4-39 and page 4-40 for discussions of the inventory methods used in the *SUA* and in the *Dynamics* project.

When your balances agree with those on page 4-44, go to the next section where you will record year-end adjusting entries.

Adjust Perpetual Inventory Records and Prepare General Journal Entries for the 1998 Year-end

The next step at the end of an accounting year before printing output is to record year-end adjusting entries. The following are the types of adjusting entries you will make:

- Physical inventory adjustment
- Depreciation expense
- Accrued interest payable
- Bad debt expense and allowance
- Cost of goods sold
- Federal income taxes

Each of the adjusting entries is explained in a section that follows. Make the adjustments in the order listed.

Adjust Perpetual Inventory Records and Post the Transactions to the General Ledger

Recall that in the *SUA* you were provided with the ending dollar balance in inventory and you adjusted to that total. That system was a periodic inventory system. *Dynamics* permits the use of a perpetual system, which provides a current inventory balance after each transaction. At year-end, a physical count is taken to adjust for obsolescence, theft, or accounting errors.

The physical count taken on December 31 indicated that there were disagreements between the physical count and the perpetual records for certain items. Management is concerned about these inventory differences, but knows that the physical count is accurate. Thus, the current perpetual records must be adjusted as follows to agree with the physical count:

Item No.	Description	Quantity on Perpetual Records	Quantity per Physical Count
B-28	Blender	92	98
FP-2	Food processor	127	124
T-104	Toaster	247	236

 Record the inventory adjustments in Dynamics.

After recording the inventory adjustment, post the transaction to the general ledger (pages 124-127 of the Reference book). Note: This step is not necessary for the remaining year-end adjusting entries because they are all prepared using the Transaction Entry window, which posts directly to the general ledger.

After the inventory adjustment is posted, you should record the remaining five year-end adjusting entries.

Record each of the remaining five year-end adjusting entries by preparing a general journal entry in Dynamics using the information provided in the next five sections.

Depreciation Expense

Depreciation expense is calculated once annually at the end of each year and recorded in the general journal as of December 31. Recall from the *SUA* that total depreciation expense for 1998 is $16,256.80. General ledger account numbers for the *Dynamics* journal entry are: #40400 (Depreciation expense) and #10900 (Accumulated depreciation).

Accrued Interest Payable

Recall from transaction #11 on page 4-32 that Waren has a $60,000 two-year note payable to First American Bank & Trust dated December 26, 1998. The stated annual interest rate on the note is 10%. The terms of the note payable call for the following payments:

- $6,000 interest payments on 12-26-99 and 12-26-00
- $60,000 principal payment on 12-26-00

Recall from the *SUA* that interest accruals are calculated using a 365-day year with the day the note was made counting as the first day. General ledger account numbers for the journal entry are: #40800 (Interest expense) and #20900 (Interest payable). Either recalculate the interest accrual now or obtain the amount from the *SUA* general journal if your entry was correct there.

Bad Debt Expense and Allowance

Recall from the *SUA* that bad debt expense is estimated once annually at the end of each year as 1/4 of one percent of net sales and is recorded in the general journal as of December 31. Also recall that Waren uses the allowance method of recording bad debt expense. General ledger account numbers for the journal entry are: #40900 (Bad debt expense) and #10300 (Allowance for doubtful accounts). Either recalculate bad debt expense now or obtain the amount from the *SUA* general journal if your entry was correct there.

> • If you need to recalculate bad debt expense, use the Reports function in *Dynamics* to determine annual net sales from the income statement. **Be sure to change the current date on your computer (top right corner of the screen) to 12/31/98 before opening the report window**.

Cost of Goods Sold

Dynamics automatically debits cost of goods sold and credits inventory for the product cost for each sale. The inventory account is also automatically updated for inventory purchases and purchases returns. Therefore, the *Dynamics* data does not include the following accounts from the *SUA*: Purchases (#30500) and Purchases Returns and Allowances (#30600). Waren treats purchase discounts taken and freight-in as a part of cost of goods sold, but records them in separate accounts during the accounting period. Therefore, these two accounts must be closed to cost of goods sold (account #30400): purchases discounts taken (#30700) and freight-in (#30800).

> • Before preparing the general journal entry, use the Inquiry function in *Dynamics* to determine the balance in each account being closed to cost of goods sold (*Inquiry* → *Financial* → *Summary*, then review the contents of the Total box for each account to be closed).

37603.05
5640.46

Federal Income Taxes

Recall that corporate income tax rates for 1998 are: 15% of the first $50,000 of income, plus 25% of the next $25,000, plus 36% of all income over $75,000. General ledger account numbers for the journal entry are: #40700 (Federal income tax expense) and #20700 (Federal income taxes payable). Either recalculate federal income tax expense now or obtain the amount from the *SUA* general journal if your entry was correct there.

- If you need to recalculate federal income tax expense, use the Reports function in *Dynamics* to determine pre-tax income from the income statement for the calculation of federal income tax expense. **Be sure the current date on your computer is 12/31/98 before opening the report window.**

Print a General Ledger Trial Balance for
Check Figures After Year-End Adjusting Entries

The trial balance on pages 4-45 and 4-46 show the correct balances in all general ledger accounts after the year-end adjusting entries are recorded.

Select a general ledger trial balance (quick summary) for Waren and print a hard copy of the 12-31-98 balances. This report will be handed in to your instructor along with year-end reports.

Compare the balances on your printed trial balance with those on pages 4-45 and 4-46. If the amounts on your printed trial balance are different, return to the year-end adjusting entries and make the necessary corrections before printing a corrected trial balance. See Appendix A in the Reference book for error correction instructions. When all errors are corrected, print a corrected trial balance.

You can also compare the amounts on your printed trial balance with those included in the *SUA* year-end adjusted trial balance (part of the year-end worksheet). All account balances should agree if your *SUA* solution was correct.

When your balances agree with those on pages 4-45 and 4-46, go to the next section where you will print financial statements and other reports.

Print Financial Statements and Other Reports

All entries have now been recorded.

🖳 *Print the following standard reports using the Reference Summary Card.* **For the two financial statements, be sure the current date is 12/31/98 before requesting the report.**

- Balance sheet
- Statement of income and retained earnings
- General journal (cross-reference report by journal entry) for December
- Account receivable aged trial balance
- Accounts payable aged trial balance
- Inventory stock status report as of 12-31-98
- Employee earnings register for 1998

🖳 *Print the following custom reports for December, following the instructions on pages 140-144 of the Reference book.*

- Sales listing
- Cash receipts listing
- Purchases listing
- Check listing
- Payroll listing

You can compare the reports printed using *Dynamics* to the manual reports you prepared in the *SUA*. The following difference exists: the sales listing report in *Dynamics* includes both credit and cash sales. In the *SUA*, cash sales are included in the cash receipts journal.

Hand in all reports to your course instructor, including the bank reconciliation reports, the customer monthly statement for Bertram Appliance, and the quick summary trial balance after year-end adjustments that you printed in previous sections.

Perform Year-end Closing Procedures

After all reports are printed, the next step is to close the general ledger for the current year. The closing process in *Dynamics* closes all income statement accounts to the retained earnings account and sets up the new fiscal year for Waren.

After all output is printed and determined to be satisfactory, complete the year-end closing procedures described in the Reference book on pages 146-149. Keep in mind that once you perform closing procedures, you can make corrections only to balance sheet accounts.

All procedures are now complete for this chapter. Now that you have completed Chapter 4, you should back up your data file for Waren Distributing, Inc. following the instructions in Chapter 1.

Account	Description	Beginning Balance	Net Change	Ending Balance
10100	Cash	$9,832.17	$54,288.98	$64,121.15
10200	Accounts Receivable	$14,724.00	$4,189.00	$18,913.00
10300	Allowance for Doubtful Accounts	($1,536.25)	$1,936.25	$400.00
10400	Inventory	$41,325.00	$19,989.00	$61,314.00
10600	Marketable Securities	$0.00	$8,000.00	$8,000.00
10800	Fixed Assets	$128,490.00	$16,068.00	$144,558.00
10900	Accumulated Depreciation	($17,017.00)	$0.00	($17,017.00)
20100	Accounts Payable	($17,398.50)	$9,367.10	($8,031.40)
20300	Federal Income Taxes Withheld	($517.82)	($368.88)	($886.70)
20400	State Unemployment Taxes Payable	($68.90)	$28.00	($40.90)
20500	Federal Unemployment Taxes Payable	($17.15)	$5.03	($12.12)
20600	F.I.C.A. Taxes Payable	($415.00)	($852.20)	($1,267.20)
20700	Federal Income Taxes Payable	($3,187.00)	$3,187.00	$0.00
21000	Notes Payable	$0.00	($60,000.00)	($60,000.00)
26000	Common Stock	($75,000.00)	$0.00	($75,000.00)
29000	Retained Earnings	($79,213.55)	$0.00	($79,213.55)
30100	Sales	$0.00	($659,289.50)	($659,289.50)
30200	Sales Returns and Allowances	$0.00	$32,070.00	$32,070.00
30300	Sales Discounts Taken	$0.00	$4,722.45	$4,722.45
30400	Cost of Goods Sold	$0.00	$440,014.00	$440,014.00
30700	Purchases Discounts Taken	$0.00	($8,397.85)	($8,397.85)
30800	Freight-in	$0.00	$9,171.00	$9,171.00
31200	Miscellaneous Revenue	$0.00	($275.00)	($275.00)
40100	Rent Expense	$0.00	$19,200.00	$19,200.00
40200	Advertising Expense	$0.00	$7,848.00	$7,848.00
40300	Office Supplies Expense	$0.00	$4,333.68	$4,333.68
40500	Wages and Salaries Expense	$0.00	$77,822.36	$77,822.36
40600	Payroll Tax Expense	$0.00	$6,839.08	$6,839.08
41000	Other Operating Expense	$0.00	$10,104.50	$10,104.50

Total Accounts: 29
    Grand Totals: $0.00 $0.00 $0.00

Account	Description	Beginning Balance	Net Change	Ending Balance
10100	Cash	$9,832.17	$54,288.98	$64,121.15
10200	Accounts Receivable	$14,724.00	$4,189.00	$18,913.00
10300	Allowance for Doubtful Accounts	($1,536.25)	$380.01	($1,156.24)
10400	Inventory	$41,325.00	$19,650.00	$60,975.00
10600	Marketable Securities	$0.00	$8,000.00	$8,000.00
10800	Fixed Assets	$128,490.00	$16,068.00	$144,558.00
10900	Accumulated Depreciation	($17,017.00)	($16,256.80)	($33,273.80)
20100	Accounts Payable	($17,398.50)	$9,367.10	($8,031.40)
20300	Federal Income Taxes Withheld	($517.82)	($368.88)	($886.70)
20400	State Unemployment Taxes Payable	($68.90)	$28.00	($40.90)
20500	Federal Unemployment Taxes Payable	($17.15)	$5.03	($12.12)
20600	F.I.C.A. Taxes Payable	($415.00)	($852.20)	($1,267.20)
20700	Federal Income Taxes Payable	($3,187.00)	($2,450.99)	($5,637.99)
20900	Interest Payable	$0.00	($98.63)	($98.63)
21000	Notes Payable	$0.00	($60,000.00)	($60,000.00)
26000	Common Stock	($75,000.00)	$0.00	($75,000.00)
29000	Retained Earnings	($79,213.55)	$0.00	($79,213.55)
30100	Sales	$0.00	($659,289.50)	($659,289.50)
30200	Sales Returns and Allowances	$0.00	$32,070.00	$32,070.00
30300	Sales Discounts Taken	$0.00	$4,722.45	$4,722.45
30400	Cost of Goods Sold	$0.00	$441,126.15	$441,126.15
30700	Purchases Discounts Taken	$0.00	$0.00	$0.00
30800	Freight-in	$0.00	$0.00	$0.00
31200	Miscellaneous Revenue	$0.00	($275.00)	($275.00)
40100	Rent Expense	$0.00	$19,200.00	$19,200.00
40200	Advertising Expense	$0.00	$7,848.00	$7,848.00
40300	Office Supplies Expense	$0.00	$4,333.68	$4,333.68
40400	Depreciation Expense	$0.00	$16,256.80	$16,256.80
40500	Wages and Salaries Expense	$0.00	$77,822.36	$77,822.36
40600	Payroll Tax Expense	$0.00	$6,839.08	$6,839.08

Account   Description

		Beginning Balance	Net Change	Ending Balance
40700	Federal Income Tax Expense	$0.00	$5,637.99	$5,637.99
40800	Interest Expense	$0.00	$98.63	$98.63
40900	Bad Debt Expense	$0.00	$1,556.24	$1,556.24
41000	Other Operating Expense	$0.00	$10,104.50	$10,104.50
Total Accounts: 34				
Grand Totals:		$0.00	$0.00	$0.00

Option C

Introduction

In this chapter, you will record the same December 16-31, 1998 transactions for Waren Distributing, Inc. that you did in the *Systems Understanding Aid for Financial Accounting (SUA)*. [Remember that date entry boxes in *Dynamics* default to your computer's current date. Thus, you will need to change them all back to 1998 dates for this project.] You will also complete other activities commonly done with accounting software and print several items to hand in to your instructor.

An important difference in this assignment compared to previous ones is the lack of detailed instructions for using *Dynamics* to record transactions and perform other activities.

If, at any time, you decide that you want to start the chapter over, you may do so by installing the *Dynamics* software again following step 1 of the installation instructions in Chapter 1. You may want to do so if you have made errors that are too difficult to correct or if you believe that you do not understand the material in this chapter.

If you install the *Dynamics* software again, all previously installed *Dynamics* software and related data files are deleted. Assuming that you backed up the data files for Chapters 2 and 3 (Jackson Supply Co.), you can restore your data files for either or both chapters by following the instructions in Chapter 1.

In recording the transactions and performing the other activities for Waren Distributing, Inc., you will need several things:

- **Optional Items from the *SUA*** (not required; all necessary information from the *SUA* has been incorporated into this chapter):
  - Instructions, Flowcharts and Ledgers book
  - Journals book
  - All year-end schedules and financial statements you prepared for Waren Distributing in the *SUA*
- **Information in this chapter**. The material instructs you what to record or do.
- **Reference Summary Card**. Use this to locate the appropriate pages in the Reference book for recording transactions or doing other activities.

- **Reference book**. Open the Reference book to the appropriate pages for the transaction you are recording or other activity you are doing and follow the instructions. In some cases, you will not have practiced using a Reference book section. You should not be concerned about this lack of practice.
- *Dynamics* **software**.

Jim Adams has recorded all transactions for the year ended 12-31-98 through December 15, 1998 using *Dynamics*. This is consistent with the *SUA*. For this assignment, you will do the following using *Dynamics*:

- Perform maintenance for inventory sales prices and costs.
- Record December 16 - 31 transactions and perform related maintenance.
- Perform December, 1998 month-end procedures.
- Record 1998 year-end adjusting entries.
- Print financial statements and other reports.
- Perform year-end closing procedures.

When you are finished, the financial statements and other results will be the same as the correct solution for the *Systems Understanding Aid*.

Perform Maintenance for Inventory Sales Prices and Costs

The price and cost list on the next page, taken from the *SUA*, reflects the current selling prices and costs for Waren's twelve products. In this section, you will compare the selling price and cost of each product to the amounts included in *Dynamics* and update *Dynamics* for any differences.

Browse Button Hint

For efficiency in moving through the inventory items, you may use the browse buttons at the top left of the window. Use the browse button to the far left to move to the first record in a list. When finished with that record, use the browse button directly to the right of center to move to the next record in the list. If needed, the browse button directly to the left of center moves to the previous record in the list and the one on the far right moves to the last record in the list. These browse buttons are available in all windows involving multiple record files.

💻 *If you are not already working in Dynamics, open the Dynamics program.*

💻 *Open Waren Distributing, Inc.*

💻 *Perform maintenance for inventory sales prices and costs for each inventory item, following the guidance on page 123 of the Reference book.* Be sure to save each inventory item changed before proceeding to the next inventory item.

PRICE AND COST LIST
AS OF DECEMBER 15, 1998

Item No.	Description	Cost	Selling Price
AC-40	Alarm Clock	$15.00	$ 18.00
B-28	Blender	38.00	53.00
CM-15	Coffee Maker	39.00	60.00
CO-22	Can Opener	16.00	20.00
EFP-510	Electric Frying Pan	29.00	40.00
EK-48	Electric Knife	18.00	25.00
FP-2	Food Processor	90.00	135.00
HD-21	Hair Dryer	19.50	27.50
I-52	Iron	24.00	33.50
M-24	Mixer	25.50	35.00
SD-21	Smoke Detector	17.00	25.00
T-104	Toaster	27.00	40.00

After you complete inventory sales price and cost maintenance, the *Dynamics* files will contain the correct default sales price and cost for each inventory item. These sales prices and costs are used for all purchases and sales of inventory between December 16 and December 31, 1998.

Record December 16-31 Transactions and Perform Related Maintenance

The transactions on pages 4-50 to 4-61 for December 16 through December 31 are the same as the transactions you recorded in the *SUA*, except where noted. Events and information that are not necessary to process the transactions in *Dynamics* have been removed. In addition, supplemental information from the *SUA* documents has been incorporated into the *Dynamics* transactions list so that you will not need the *SUA* transactions list or the *SUA* documents to complete this section. The transactions should be dealt with in the order listed. Some of the transactions must be recorded whereas others require only maintenance.

In dealing with each transaction or maintenance task, the information you have already learned about *Dynamics* during Familiarization and Practice are used. You should use the *Dynamics* Reference book and information from prior chapters to the extent you need it. Also, if you want to check whether information was recorded, it is easy to determine by using the Inquiry function. You can also compare each transaction you record in *Dynamics* to the result you obtained when you did the *SUA*, although this is not required. Use the *SUA* journals book for this comparison.

Recall that most transaction entry windows in *Dynamics* provide access to an additional window for entering general ledger account distributions. All default general ledger distribution accounts are correct for Waren's December 16-31 transactions unless otherwise noted on pages 4-50 to 4-61.

WAREN DISTRIBUTING TRANSACTIONS FOR DECEMBER 16-31, 1998

Record each of the following transactions (#1-30) using Dynamics.

- Hints are provided in boxed areas like this.

Use care in recording each transaction. **At a minimum, you should follow** *each step* **in the Quick Reference Table for each transaction**. It may take slightly more time, but it will almost certainly help you avoid serious errors. Find the appropriate Quick Reference Table for each transaction or other activity by using the Reference Summary Card.

Transaction#   December

1   16   **Prepare a purchase order:** Ordered the following inventory on account from Super Electric Co., Housewares Division, using purchase order No. 335. The goods will be received at the warehouse at a later date. The purchase order total is $20,600.

Units	Item #	Description
150	CO-22	Can opener
250	EFP-510	Electric frying pan
125	EK-48	Electric knife
250	HD-21	Hair dryer
150	M-24	Mixer

2 | 18 **Make a credit sale:** Received customer purchase order No. TX20901 in the mail from Fritter Appliance, approved their credit, prepared invoice No. 730 totaling $7,315, and shipped the goods from the warehouse. All goods ordered were shipped as follows:

Units	Item #	Description
30	AC-40	Alarm clock
50	CO-22	Can opener
25	FP-2	Food processor
60	T-104	Toaster

3 | 20 **Change an employee record (employee maintenance):** Increased employee salary and wage rates, effective December 15. Recall that for hourly employees, overtime is paid at 1.5 times the regular hourly rate. There were no changes in filing status or withholding allowances. *Note: Ignore the federal income tax withholding amount changes in the SUA.*

Employee	New Salary/Wage Rate
Ray Kramer	$2,400, semimonthly
Jim Adams	$9.50 per hour
Nancy Ford	$8.40 per hour

- Select the Pay Codes button at the bottom of the Employee Maintenance-USA window to change pay rates.
- You will make a total of five pay rate changes for the three employees, including overtime pay rates: two each for the two hourly employees and one for the salaried employee. Save each pay rate change after entering it.
- When asked, "Do you want to roll down this rate change to all pay codes based on this pay code?", click "No."
- Remember to use the browse buttons to move through the employee records.

---

4 | 23 **Write-off an uncollectible account receivable:** Received legal notification from Benson, Rosenbrook and Martinson, P.C., attorneys at law, that Okemos Housewares had filed bankruptcy and is unable to pay any of its outstanding debts to its suppliers. The $850 balance remaining on invoice #718 should therefore be written off as uncollectible. Recall that Waren uses the allowance method for recording bad debt expense.

5   23   **Collect an outstanding account receivable and make a bank deposit:** Received check No. 1643 for $2,500 from Bertram Appliance in partial payment of sales invoice No. 728, and deposited the check.

> • After recording the cash receipt, record the deposit into the bank on the same day using the Bank Deposit Entry window (see pages 46-48 of the Reference book).

6   23   **Receive goods on a sales return:** Hanover Hardware returned 20 mixers and 20 alarm clocks that were originally purchased on invoice No. 729A. The goods are to be returned to "On Hand" status. Waren previously authorized Hanover Hardware by phone to return the goods for credit against their account balance. Hanover's return request No. 6256 was received with the goods. Sales return document CM 42 was issued for $1,060 and applied to invoice No. 729A.

Note: Invoice No. 729 from the SUA was split into two transactions in Dynamics: invoice Nos. 729 and 729A. This was done to simplify the use of Dynamics.

> • **Remember to apply sales return document CM 42 to invoice No. 729A** (*not* invoice No. 729). See steps R-X in the quick reference table.

7   23   **Collect an outstanding account receivable and make a bank deposit:** Received and deposited check No. 6401 for $642.88 from Hanover Hardware for payment in full of invoice No. 729. The early payment discount taken by Hanover was $13.12.

> • Remember to apply the cash receipt to invoice No. 729, *not* No. 729A.
> • After recording the cash receipt, record the deposit into the bank on the same day using the Bank Deposit Entry window (see pages 46-48 of the Reference book).

8	24	**Receive goods from a purchase order:** Received merchandise from Super Electric as listed on purchase order No. 335, along with invoice #18719 totaling $17,675. The payment terms on the invoice are 2/10, Net 30. All merchandise listed on the purchase order was delivered in good condition and in the quantities ordered, except that only 100 hair dryers (Item No. HD 21) were received. The goods were placed immediately in the inventory warehouse.

> - Be sure to select "Shipment/Invoice," not "Shipment," in step B of the quick reference table.
> - Be sure to do step G, click the Auto-Rcv button.
> - You must enter account #10400, Inventory, as the Purchases account (Type = PURCH) in the Purchasing Distribution Entry window because the default account number will be blank.

9	24	**Purchase goods or services without a purchase order:** Received freight bill No. 78219 for $660 from Interstate Motor Freight and immediately issued check No. 257 for payment in full. The freight bill relates to the merchandise received from purchase order No. 335. The payment terms on the freight bill are Net 30.

> - Be sure to enter the payment information for check No. 257. See step I in the quick reference table.

| 10 | 24 | **Make a cash sale and make a bank deposit:** Received and deposited check No. 5418 for $12,500 and customer purchase order No. 137592 in the mail from Redwood Fixtures for a cash sale. The goods were shipped from the warehouse and the cash sale was processed and recorded using invoice No. C-36. All goods ordered were shipped as follows: |

Units	Item #	Description
50	CM-15	Coffee maker
100	EFP-510	Electric frying pans
200	HD-21	Hair dryers

> - Do not forget steps N-S in the quick reference table (enter customer's payment information) or you will not be able to deposit the check.
> - After recording the cash sale, record the deposit into the bank on the same day using the Bank Deposit Entry window (see pages 46-48 of the Reference book).

| 11 | 24 | **Prepare a purchase order:** Ordered the following inventory on account from Super Electric Co., Housewares Division, using purchase order No. 336. The goods will be received at the warehouse at a later date. The purchase order total is $7,500. |

Note: This transaction differs slightly from the SUA. For simplicity of entering the transaction in Dynamics, the December 30th purchase return in the SUA has been netted with the December 26th receipt of goods for purchase order No. 336. Therefore, the net amount of goods needs to be entered during the preparation of purchase order No. 336.

Units	Item #	Description
25	FP-2	Food Processor
75	SD-21	Smoke Detector
50	CM-15	Coffee Maker
75	T-104	Toaster

12   26   **Receive a miscellaneous cash receipt and make a bank deposit:** Borrowed and deposited $60,000 from First American Bank & Trust by issuing a two-year note payable. Check No. 545 for $60,000 was received and deposited.

> - The credit portion of the transaction should be posted to account #21000, Notes Payable.
> - After recording the cash receipt, record the deposit into the bank on the same day using the Bank Deposit Entry window (see pages 46-48 of the Reference book).

13   26   **Receive goods from a purchase order:** Received, and recorded as an expense, office supplies from Chicago Office Supply as listed on purchase order No. 334, which is shown as an open purchase order in *Dynamics*. Chicago Office Supply's vendor invoice No. 2294 was received with the goods, totaling $231.40 including sales tax. The payment terms on the invoice are "Upon receipt." All supplies ordered on purchase order No. 334 were received in good condition and taken to the warehouse.

> - Be sure to select "Shipment/Invoice," not "Shipment," in step B of the quick reference table.
> - You must enter account #40300, Office Supplies Expense, as the Purchases account (Type = PURCH) in the Purchasing Distribution Entry window because the default account number will be blank.

14   26   **Make a credit sale:** Made a special promotional sale on account to Saginaw Sales & Service, using invoice No. 731, totaling $2,700. For the promotion, Waren agreed to a 10% reduction in the selling prices of the items sold. Saginaw did not submit a purchase order for the sale. The following goods were shipped from the warehouse for this sale:

Units	Item No.	Description
50	CM-15	Coffee Maker

> • Use the Markdown expansion button to record the reduction in the sales price for the inventory items sold.

Note: Invoice No. 731 from the SUA was split into two transactions in Dynamics: invoice Nos. 731 and 731A. Invoice No. 731A will be recorded in transaction #16.

15   26   **Change a customer record (customer maintenance):** Changed the payment terms for Saginaw Sales & Service (customer ID 410) from Net 30 to 2/10, Net 30. You are to change Saginaw's customer record to reflect this change.

> • Be sure to save the revised customer record after making the payment terms change.

16   26   **Make a credit sale:** Made another special promotional sale on account to Saginaw Sales & Service, using invoice No. 731A, totaling $8,235. For the promotion, Waren agreed to a 10% reduction in the selling prices of the items sold. Saginaw did not submit a purchase order for the sale. The following goods were shipped from the warehouse for this sale:

Units	Item No.	Description
175	AC-40	Alarm Clock
100	CM-15	Coffee Maker

> • Use the Markdown expansion button to record the reduction in the sales price for the inventory items sold.

17   26   **Receive goods from a purchase order:** Received merchandise from Super Electric as listed on purchase order No. 336, along with invoice #19413 totaling $7,500. The payment terms on the invoice are 2/10, Net 30. All merchandise listed on the purchase order was delivered in good condition and were placed immediately in the inventory warehouse. *Note: Recall from page 4-54 that the December 26th receipt of goods and the December 30th purchase return from the SUA are netted in this project.*

- Be sure to select "Shipment/Invoice," not "Shipment," in step B of the quick reference table.
- You must enter account #10400, Inventory, as the Purchases account (Type = PURCH) in the Purchasing Distribution Entry window because the default account number will be blank.

---

18   27   **Receive a miscellaneous cash receipt and make a bank deposit:** Received check No. 3002 from Central Brokerage for $622 of dividend income. The dividends were earned on various common stocks in the marketable securities general ledger account.

- The credit portion of the transaction should be posted to account #31100, Interest/Dividend Income.
- After recording the cash receipt, record the deposit into the bank on the same day using the Bank Deposit Entry window (see pages 46-48 of the Reference book).

---

19   27   **Prepare a general journal entry:** Sold an office desk to an employee, Nancy Ford, for $120. Nancy will pay this amount to Waren in January of 1999. The desk was purchased for a cost of $930 on September 30, 1992. The desk was fully depreciated at the end of 1997. Either recompute the amounts for this transaction now, or obtain the correct information from the *SUA* general journal.

- The receivable from Nancy Ford should be posted to account #10210 — Accounts Receivable from Employees and the gain or loss should be posted to account #30900 — Gain/Loss on Sale of Fixed Assets.

---

20   27   **Receive goods on a sales return:** Received a return for credit of 50 coffee makers, item CM-15, from Saginaw Sales & Service. These items were originally sold on invoice No. 731 at a 10% promotional discount on December 26 (see transaction #14 on page 4-56). The items were returned to "On Hand" status. No document was received from Saginaw with the return. Sales return document CM 43 was issued for $2,700 and applied to invoice No. 731.

- Be sure to consider the effects of the promotional markdown when recording the sales return.
- In the Invoice Distribution Entry window, you need to change the general ledger account for the $300 markdown credit (Type = MARK) from account #30100, Sales, to account #30200, Sales Returns and Allowances.
- **Remember to apply sales return document CM 43 to invoice No. 731** (*not* invoice No. 731A). See steps R-X in the quick reference table.

21   30   **Pay an outstanding vendor's invoice:** Issued check No. 258 for $17,321.50 to Super Electric for payment in full of invoice No. 18719 for goods received December 24. The early payment discount taken by Waren was $353.50.

22   30   **Collect an outstanding account receivable and make a bank deposit:** Received check No. 1450 for $8,070.30 from Saginaw Sales & Service in payment of invoice No. 731A (see transaction #16 on page 4-56 for the original sale transaction). The early payment discount taken by Saginaw was $164.70.

- Remember to apply the cash receipt to invoice No. 731A, *not* No. 731.
- After recording the cash receipt, record the deposit into the bank on the same day using the Bank Deposit Entry window (see pages 46-48 of the Reference book).

23   31   **Pay employees:** Finished the payroll for the semimonthly pay period December 16-31, 1998, and issued checks No. 259-261 as follows:

Employee	Check#	Gross pay	Federal Tax Withheld	FICA Tax Withheld	Net pay
Ray Kramer	259	$2,400.00	$348.19	$192.00	$1,859.81
Jim Adams	260	$ 944.49	$ 94.95	$ 75.56	$ 773.98
Nancy Ford	261	$ 884.90	$ 47.11	$ 70.79	$ 767.00

- For Nancy Ford and Jim Adams (hourly employees), ignore the distinction between regular and overtime hours and earnings from the *SUA* when recording the payroll checks in *Dynamics*. Regular and overtime earnings are reflected in the Gross pay amounts shown above, and both should be entered under the HOUR pay code in the Payroll Manual Check Transaction Entry - USA window.

24   31   **Receive goods from a purchase order:** Received a computer from Chicago Office Supply ordered on Waren's purchase order No. 332, which is shown as an open purchase order in *Dynamics*. Also received vendor's invoice No. 2305 from Chicago Office Supply, totaling $7,800 including sales tax. The payment terms on the invoice are "Upon receipt." The computer was received in new and undamaged condition in the warehouse. After it was unpacked and tested, it was taken directly to the office. It was not paid for.

- Be sure to select "Shipment/Invoice," not "Shipment," in step B of the quick reference table.
- Be sure to do step G, click the Auto-Rcv button.
- You must enter account #10800, Fixed Assets, *twice* in the Purchasing Distribution Entry window: once for the Purchases debit (Type = PURCH) and once for the Tax debit (Type = TAX). One of the default account numbers is blank and one is incorrect for a fixed asset purchase.

25   **31**   **Purchase goods or services without a purchase order:** Received vendor invoice No. 892 for $1,050 from the Chicago Daily Times for newspaper advertisements Waren ran during the Christmas season and immediately issued check No. 262 for payment in full. The payment terms on the invoice are "Upon receipt."

> - Be sure to enter the payment information for check No. 262. See step I in the quick reference table.

26   **31**   **Receive a miscellaneous cash receipt and make a bank deposit:** Sold 100 shares of Franklin Corporation common stock for $27.50 per share. The shares were originally purchased on July 8, 1998 for $22.00 per share plus a commission of $66.00. Central Brokerage retained a $110.00 commission on the sale and forwarded check No. 3175 for the net sale proceeds to Waren of $2,640. Either recompute the amounts for this transaction now or obtain the correct amounts from the *SUA* cash receipts journal.

> - The following accounts should be used for this transaction: #10100 (Cash), #10600 (Marketable Securities) and #31000 (Gain/Loss on Sale of Marketable Securities).
> - After recording the cash receipt, record the deposit into the bank on the same day using the Bank Deposit Entry window (see pages 46-48 of the Reference book).

27   **31**   **Pay an outstanding vendor's invoice:** Issued No. 263 for $7,350 to pay Super Electric's invoice No. 19413 for items received on December 26. The early payment discount taken by Waren was $150.

28   31   **Purchase goods or services without a purchase order:** Loaned $6,000 to Maple Valley Electric by issuing a three-year note receivable. The funds were loaned by issuing check No. 264. Interest payments are due on December 31 of each year, beginning in 1999, and no interest is receivable at 12/31/98.

- Since no document number exists, type [NOTE] in the Document Number box.
- Be sure to enter the payment information for check No. 264. See step I in the quick reference table.
- The debit portion of the transaction should be posted to account #11000, Notes Receivable.

29   31   **Purchase goods or services without a purchase order:** Issued check No. 265 to First American Bank & Trust for $12,000 for partial payment on the bank note, which included no payment for interest. The terms on the back of the bank note stipulate that prepayments such as this one can be made without early payment penalty. For purposes of your year-end adjusting journal entry for interest, note that this payment will not reach the bank until 1999.

- Type the loan number, 6X-28941, in the Document Number box.
- The debit portion of the transaction should be posted to account #21000, Notes Payable.
- Be sure to enter the payment information for check No. 265. See step I in the quick reference table.

30   31   **Purchase goods or services without a purchase order:** Issued check No. 266 to Worldwide Management for $1,650 in payment of invoice #2476 covering the January, 1999 rent.

- Be sure to enter the payment information for check No. 266. See step I in the quick reference table.
- The debit portion of the transaction should be posted to account #10500, Prepaid Expenses. You will have to edit the Payables Transaction Distribution Entry window for this change.

Perform December 1998 Month-end Procedures

Because many of Waren's month-end procedures are done automatically by *Dynamics*, the only month-end procedures you will need to perform are:

- Accrue monthly unemployment taxes.
- Prepare the December bank reconciliation.
- Post December 16-31 transactions to the general ledger.
- Perform accounts receivable aging and print a customer monthly statement.

Prepare a General Journal Entry for Monthly Unemployment Taxes

Recall from the *SUA* that only one of Waren's employees, Nancy Ford, remains subject to federal and state unemployment taxes as of December, 1998. The amounts for Nancy Ford for December are:

SUTA (account #20400)	$40.90
FUTA (account #20500)	12.12
Total (account #40600)	$53.02

Note that all information necessary for the journal entry is also included in the *SUA* general journal. *Note: Ignore the employer's F.I.C.A. portion of the entry in the SUA general journal; Dynamics automatically calculates this amount for each pay check.*

⌨ *Record a general journal entry in Dynamics for the accrual of December's federal and state unemployment taxes.*

- Be sure that Account #40600 is the debit.

Prepare the December Bank Reconciliation

Check Figure for Your Cash Balance

Before starting the December bank reconciliation, be sure that your cash balance is correct by completing the following steps:

- 💻 *Click Inquiry → Financial → Checkbook Register to open the Checkbook Register Inquiry window.*
- 💻 *Select FIRST (First American Bank & Trust) in the Checkbook ID box.*

Review the contents of the Current Balance box. The balance should be $48,481.95. If it is not, the first thing to check is whether you remembered to record a bank deposit for transactions #5, 7, 10, 12, 17, 21, and 25. If you forgot to record any or all bank deposits, record them now following the Reference book instructions on pages 46-48.

If you have recorded all bank deposits and your cash balance is still wrong in the Checkbook Register Inquiry window, return to the December 16-31 transactions to locate and correct any other errors before starting the bank reconciliation. When your cash balance is correct, continue with the requirements that follow.

Bank Reconciliation Information, Process, and Printing

As you process through the December reconciliation steps (computer symbols), do them in order and *do not click on the Reconcile button until told to do so*. You will need to print some reports first, and those reports will not be available after you click on the Reconcile button.

The following information is taken from the December bank statement and the November bank reconciliation, none of which is included in these materials:

- The December 31, 1998 bank statement balance is $27,768.44.

- The following checks have not cleared the bank as of December 31: checks #217, and #257 through #266.

- The following four deposits have not cleared the bank as of December 31:

> (1) The December 26 deposit of loan proceeds.
> (2) The December 27 deposit of dividend income.
> (3) The December 30 deposit from Saginaw Sales & Service.
> (4) The December 31 deposit from the Franklin stock sale.

- A service charge of $28.50 is included on the December bank statement. *Note: The bank service charge should be posted to account #41000 — Other operating expense.*

🖥 *Prepare the December bank reconciliation, **but do not click the Reconcile button yet** (step R in the quick reference table on page 92 of the Reference book) because you need to print the reconciliation first.* The cutoff date for the bank reconciliation is December 31, 1998.

🖥 *When the reconciliation is correct, click File → Print to open the Print Reconciliation Reports window.*

🖥 *Remove the check marks next to the following reports so that they do not print: Bank Adjustments Edit List and Marked Transactions Report. Then click the OK button.* A Report Destination window will open for the first checked report, Reconciliation Edit List.

🖥 *Select Screen as the output destination and click OK.* Next you will get the Report Destination window for the Outstanding Transactions Report.

🖥 *Select Screen again and click OK.* This will bring up the screen output for the first report selected, Reconcile Journal.

🖥 *Click the print button in the top left corner of this window to print the reconciliation. Click OK at the next window asking about number of copies.*

🖥 *Repeat the previous step for the next output screen to come up, Outstanding Transactions Report.*

🖥 *Review your printed output for accuracy and acceptability.* These reports will be handed in to your instructor along with year-end reports.

🖥 *Click the Reconcile button in the Select Bank Transactions window (step R in the quick reference table on page 92 of the Reference book).*

Post December 16 - 31 Transactions to the General Ledger

Waren's accountant posted all transactions to the general ledger through December 15, 1998. You are to post the December 16-31 transactions to the general ledger.

🖥 *Post the December 16-31 transactions using the instructions in the Reference book on pages 124-127.* Although you have not practiced posting, it is easy to do when following the Reference book.

Age Accounts Receivable and
Print Customer Monthly Statements

Before customer monthly statements can be prepared, you must perform the *Dynamics* aging routine for accounts receivable. Before you do so, read the Age Accounts Receivable and Print Customer Monthly Statements Overview on page 128 of the Reference book.

💻 *Complete the accounts receivable aging process as of 12-31-98 for Waren, (steps A-E in the quick reference table on page 128).*

At the end of each month, Waren sends monthly statements to all customers with an outstanding balance. For this section, you are to print a hard copy of the December monthly statement for Bertram Appliance.

💻 *Print a hard copy of the December monthly statement for Bertram Appliance, using the Reference book instructions on pages 131-132 (steps F-N in the quick reference table on page 128).*

Print a General Ledger Trial Balance for
Check Figures Prior to Year-End Adjusting Entries

The trial balance on pages 4-72 and 4-73 shows the correct balances in all general ledger accounts after the December month-end procedures are completed.

💻 *Select a general ledger trial balance (quick summary) for Waren, and print a hard copy of the 12-31-98 balances using the Reference book instructions on pages 134-139 and the Select Reports section of the Reference Summary Card.* Note: Due to a small font size, you cannot view the trial balance numbers on the screen before printing.

Compare the amounts on your printed trial balance with those on pages 4-72 and 4-73. If any amounts are different, return to the December 16-31 transactions and the month-end procedures you processed in *Dynamics* and make the necessary corrections. See Appendix A in the Reference book for error correction instructions. When all errors are corrected, print a corrected trial balance.

You can also compare the amounts on your printed trial balance with those included in the *SUA* year-end unadjusted trial balance (part of the year-end worksheet). All account balances should agree if your solution to the *SUA* was correct except inventory-related accounts. Inventory-related account balances do not agree because of the use of different inventory methods. The balances will agree after adjusting entries are completed. See pages 4-66 to 4-67 and page 4-68 for discussions of the inventory methods used in the *SUA* and in the *Dynamics* project.

When your balances agree with those on pages 4-72 and 4-73 go to the next section where you will record year-end adjusting entries.

Adjust Perpetual Inventory Records and Prepare General Journal Entries for the 1998 Year-end

The next step at the end of an accounting year before printing output is to record year-end adjusting entries. The following are the types of adjusting entries you will make:

- Physical inventory adjustment
- Depreciation expense
- Accrued interest payable
- Bad debt expense and allowance
- Cost of goods sold
- Federal income taxes

Each of the adjusting entries is explained in a section that follows. Make the adjustments in the order listed.

Adjust Perpetual Inventory Records and Post the Transactions to the General Ledger

Recall that in the *SUA* you were provided with the ending dollar balance in inventory and you adjusted to that total. That system was a periodic inventory system. *Dynamics* permits the use of a perpetual system, which provides a current inventory balance after each transaction. At year-end, a physical count is taken to adjust for obsolescence, theft, or accounting errors.

The physical count taken on December 31 indicated that there were disagreements between the physical count and the perpetual records for certain items. Management is concerned about these inventory differences, but believes that the physical count is accurate. Thus, the current perpetual records must be adjusted as follows to agree with the physical count:

Item No.	Description	Quantity on Perpetual Records	Quantity per Physical Count
B-28	Blender	92	98
FP-2	Food processor	127	124
T-104	Toaster	247	236

Record the inventory adjustments in Dynamics.

After recording the inventory adjustment, post the transaction to the general ledger (pages 124-127 of the Reference book). Note: This step is not necessary for the remaining year-end adjusting entries because they are all prepared using the Transaction Entry window, which posts directly to the general ledger.

After the inventory adjustment is posted, you should record the remaining five year-end adjusting entries.

Record each of the remaining five year-end adjusting entries by preparing a general journal entry in Dynamics using the information provided in the next five sections.

Depreciation Expense

Depreciation expense is calculated once annually at the end of each year and recorded in the general journal as of December 31. Recall from the *SUA* that total depreciation expense for 1998 was $16,256.80. General ledger account numbers for the *Dynamics* journal entry are: #40400 (Depreciation Expense) and #10900 (Accumulated Depreciation).

Accrued Interest Payable

Recall from transaction #12 on page 4-55 that Waren has a $60,000 two-year note payable to First American Bank & Trust dated December 26, 1998. The stated annual interest rate on the note is 10%. The terms of the note payable call for the following payments:

- $6,000 interest payments on 12-26-99 and 12-26-00
- $60,000 principal payment on 12-26-00

Recall from the *SUA* that interest accruals are calculated using a 365-day year with the day the note was made counting as the first day. General ledger account numbers for the journal entry are: #40800 (Interest expense) and #20900 (Interest payable). Either recalculate the interest accrual now or obtain the amount from the *SUA* general journal if your entry was correct there.

Bad Debt Expense and Allowance

Recall from the *SUA* that bad debt expense is estimated once annually at the end of each year as 1/4 of one percent of net sales and is recorded in the general journal as of December 31. Also recall that Waren uses the allowance method of recording bad debt expense. General ledger account numbers for the journal entry are: #40900 (Bad debt expense) and #10300 (Allowance for doubtful accounts). Either recalculate bad debt expense now or obtain the amount from the *SUA* general journal if your entry was correct there.

> • If you need to recalculate bad debt expense, use the Reports function in *Dynamics* to determine annual net sales from the income statement. **Be sure to change the current date on your computer (top right corner of the screen) to 12/31/98 before opening the report window**.

Cost of Goods Sold

Dynamics automatically debits cost of goods sold and credits inventory for the product cost for each sale. The inventory account is also automatically updated for inventory purchases and purchases returns. Therefore, the *Dynamics* data does not include the following accounts from the *SUA*: Purchases (#30500) and Purchases Returns and Allowances (#30600). Waren treats purchase discounts taken and freight-in as a part of cost of goods sold, but records them in separate accounts during the accounting period. Therefore, these two accounts must be closed to cost of goods sold (account #30400): purchases discounts taken (#30700) and freight-in (#30800).

> • Before preparing the general journal entry, use the Inquiry function in *Dynamics* to determine the balance in each account being closed to cost of goods sold (*Inquiry* → *Financial* → *Summary*, then review the contents of the Total box for each account to be closed).

Federal Income Taxes

Recall that corporate income tax rates for 1998 are: 15% of the first $50,000 of income, plus 25% of the next $25,000, plus 36% of all income over $75,000. General ledger account numbers for the journal entry are: #40700 (Federal income tax expense) and #20700 (Federal income taxes payable). Either recalculate federal income tax expense now or obtain the amount from the *SUA* general journal if your entry was correct there.

> ● If you need to recalculate federal income tax expense, use the Reports function in *Dynamics* to determine pre-tax income from the income statement for the calculation of federal income tax expense. **Be sure the current date on your computer is 12/31/98 before opening the report window.**

Print a General Ledger Trial Balance for Check Figures After Year-End Adjusting Entries

The trial balance on pages 4-74 and 4-75 show the correct balances in all general ledger accounts after the year-end adjusting entries are recorded.

Select a general ledger trial balance (quick summary) for Waren and print a hard copy of the 12-31-98 balances. This report will be handed in to your instructor along with year-end reports.

Compare the balances on your printed trial balance with those on pages 4-74 and 4-75. If the amounts on your printed trial balance are different, return to the year-end adjusting entries and make the necessary corrections before printing a corrected trial balance. See Appendix A in the Reference book for error correction instructions. When all errors are corrected, print a corrected trial balance.

You can also compare the amounts on your printed trial balance with those included in the *SUA* year-end adjusted trial balance (part of the year-end worksheet). All account balances should agree if your *SUA* solution was correct.

When your balances agree with those on pages 4-74 and 4-75, go to the next section where you will print financial statements and other reports.

Print Financial Statements and Other Reports

All entries have now been recorded.

Print the following standard reports using the Reference Summary Card. **For the two financial statements, be sure the current date is 12/31/98 before requesting the report.**

- Balance sheet
- Statement of income and retained earnings
- General journal (cross-reference report by journal entry) for December
- Account receivable aged trial balance
- Accounts payable aged trial balance
- Inventory stock status report as of 12-31-98
- Employee earnings register for 1998

Print the following custom reports for December, following the instructions on pages 140-144 of the Reference book.

- Sales listing
- Cash receipts listing
- Purchases listing
- Check listing
- Payroll listing

You can compare the reports printed using *Dynamics* to the manual reports you prepared in the *SUA*. The following difference exists: the sales listing report in *Dynamics* includes both credit and cash sales. In the *SUA*, cash sales are included in the cash receipts journal.

Hand in all reports to your course instructor, including the bank reconciliation reports, customer monthly statement for Bertram Appliance, and the quick summary trial balance after year-end adjustments that you printed in previous sections.

Perform Year-end Closing Procedures

After all reports are printed, the next step is to close the general ledger for the current year. The closing process in *Dynamics* closes all income statement accounts to the retained earnings account and sets up the new fiscal year for Waren.

After all output is printed and determined to be satisfactory, complete the year-end closing procedures described in the Reference book on pages 146-149. Keep in mind that once you perform closing procedures, you can make corrections only to balance sheet accounts.

All procedures are now complete for this chapter. Now that you have completed Chapter 4, you should back up your data file for Waren Distributing, Inc. following the instructions in Chapter 1.

Account	Description	Beginning Balance	Net Change	Ending Balance
10100	Cash	$9,832.17	$38,621.28	$48,453.45
10200	Accounts Receivable	$14,724.00	$4,189.00	$18,913.00
10210	Accounts Receivable from Employees	$0.00	$120.00	$120.00
10300	Allowance for Doubtful Accounts	($1,536.25)	$1,936.25	$400.00
10400	Inventory	$41,325.00	$20,964.00	$62,289.00
10500	Prepaid Expenses	$0.00	$1,650.00	$1,650.00
10600	Marketable Securities	$0.00	$5,734.00	$5,734.00
10800	Fixed Assets	$128,490.00	$15,138.00	$143,628.00
10900	Accumulated Depreciation	($17,017.00)	$930.00	($16,087.00)
11000	Notes Receivable	$0.00	$6,000.00	$6,000.00
20100	Accounts Payable	($17,398.50)	$9,367.10	($8,031.40)
20300	Federal Income Taxes Withheld	($517.82)	($368.88)	($886.70)
20400	State Unemployment Taxes Payable	($68.90)	$28.00	($40.90)
20500	Federal Unemployment Taxes Payable	($17.15)	$5.03	($12.12)
20600	F.I.C.A. Taxes Payable	($415.00)	($852.20)	($1,267.20)
20700	Federal Income Taxes Payable	($3,187.00)	$3,187.00	$0.00
21000	Notes Payable	$0.00	($48,000.00)	($48,000.00)
26000	Common Stock	($75,000.00)	$0.00	($75,000.00)
29000	Retained Earnings	($79,213.55)	$0.00	($79,213.55)
30100	Sales	$0.00	($670,224.50)	($670,224.50)
30200	Sales Returns and Allowances	$0.00	$34,770.00	$34,770.00
30300	Sales Discounts Taken	$0.00	$4,887.15	$4,887.15
30400	Cost of Goods Sold	$0.00	$446,539.00	$446,539.00
30700	Purchases Discounts Taken	$0.00	($8,547.85)	($8,547.85)
30800	Freight-in	$0.00	$9,171.00	$9,171.00
30900	Gain/Loss on Sale of Fixed Assets	$0.00	($120.00)	($120.00)
31000	Gain/Loss on Sale of Marketable Securities	$0.00	($374.00)	($374.00)
31100	Interest/Dividend Income	$0.00	($622.00)	($622.00)
31200	Miscellaneous Revenue	$0.00	($275.00)	($275.00)
40100	Rent Expense	$0.00	$19,200.00	$19,200.00

Account	Description	Beginning Balance	Net Change	Ending Balance
40200	Advertising Expense			
		$0.00	$7,848.00	$7,848.00
40300	Office Supplies Expense			
		$0.00	$4,333.68	$4,333.68
40500	Wages and Salaries Expense			
		$0.00	$77,822.36	$77,822.36
40600	Payroll Tax Expense			
		$0.00	$6,839.08	$6,839.08
41000	Other Operating Expense			
		$0.00	$10,104.50	$10,104.50
Total Accounts: 35				
Grand Totals:		$0.00	$0.00	$0.00

Account	Description	Beginning Balance	Net Change	Ending Balance
10100	Cash	$9,832.17	$38,621.28	$48,453.45
10200	Accounts Receivable	$14,724.00	$4,189.00	$18,913.00
10210	Accounts Receivable from Employees	$0.00	$120.00	$120.00
10300	Allowance for Doubtful Accounts	($1,536.25)	$359.83	($1,176.42)
10400	Inventory	$41,325.00	$20,625.00	$61,950.00
10500	Prepaid Expenses	$0.00	$1,650.00	$1,650.00
10600	Marketable Securities	$0.00	$5,734.00	$5,734.00
10800	Fixed Assets	$128,490.00	$15,138.00	$143,628.00
10900	Accumulated Depreciation	($17,017.00)	($15,326.80)	($32,343.80)
11000	Notes Receivable	$0.00	$6,000.00	$6,000.00
20100	Accounts Payable	($17,398.50)	$9,367.10	($8,031.40)
20300	Federal Income Taxes Withheld	($517.82)	($368.88)	($886.70)
20400	State Unemployment Taxes Payable	($68.90)	$28.00	($40.90)
20500	Federal Unemployment Taxes Payable	($17.15)	$5.03	($12.12)
20600	F.I.C.A. Taxes Payable	($415.00)	($852.20)	($1,267.20)
20700	Federal Income Taxes Payable	($3,187.00)	($2,869.66)	($6,056.66)
20900	Interest Payable	$0.00	($98.63)	($98.63)
21000	Notes Payable	$0.00	($48,000.00)	($48,000.00)
26000	Common Stock	($75,000.00)	$0.00	($75,000.00)
29000	Retained Earnings	($79,213.55)	$0.00	($79,213.55)
30100	Sales	$0.00	($670,224.50)	($670,224.50)
30200	Sales Returns and Allowances	$0.00	$34,770.00	$34,770.00
30300	Sales Discounts Taken	$0.00	$4,887.15	$4,887.15
30400	Cost of Goods Sold	$0.00	$447,501.15	$447,501.15
30700	Purchases Discounts Taken	$0.00	$0.00	$0.00
30800	Freight-in	$0.00	$0.00	$0.00
30900	Gain/Loss on Sale of Fixed Assets	$0.00	($120.00)	($120.00)
31000	Gain/Loss on Sale of Marketable Securities	$0.00	($374.00)	($374.00)
31100	Interest/Dividend Income	$0.00	($622.00)	($622.00)
31200	Miscellaneous Revenue	$0.00	($275.00)	($275.00)

Account   Description

                                        Beginning Balance   Net Change   Ending Balance
----

40100   Rent Expense
                                                $0.00 $19,200.00 $19,200.00
40200   Advertising Expense
                                                $0.00 $7,848.00 $7,848.00
40300   Office Supplies Expense
                                                $0.00 $4,333.68 $4,333.68
40400   Depreciation Expense
                                                $0.00 $16,256.80 $16,256.80
40500   Wages and Salaries Expense
                                                $0.00 $77,822.36 $77,822.36
40600   Payroll Tax Expense
                                                $0.00 $6,839.08 $6,839.08
40700   Federal Income Tax Expense
                                                $0.00 $6,056.66 $6,056.66
40800   Interest Expense
                                                $0.00 $98.63 $98.63
40900   Bad Debt Expense
                                                $0.00 $1,576.42 $1,576.42
41000   Other Operating Expense
                                                $0.00 $10,104.50 $10,104.50

Total Accounts: 40
    Grand Totals: $0.00 $0.00 $0.00

This page is intentionally blank.

CHAPTER 5

Using *Dynamics* for
a Large Company

Introduction

The companies you worked with in Chapters 2 through 4, Jackson Supply Company and Waren Distributing, Inc., are small companies with relatively noncomplex structures and transactions. While *Dynamics* is more than sufficient to accommodate small companies, the program is also designed for larger and more complex entities. In this chapter, you will explore how *Dynamics* operates for a large multinational computer and electronics distributor, The World Online, Incorporated. You will also record a few transactions for the company and print a Profit and Loss report to hand in to your instructor. You will observe that the differences are not significant except for the number of such things as customers and vendors.

In addition to its main office and warehouse in Chicago, The World Online, Inc. also has offices in Canada (Winnipeg, Manitoba) and Sydney, Australia. The general ledger is organized around the company's six departments and consists of 430 posting accounts.

If, at any time, you decide that you want to start the chapter over, you may do so by installing the *Dynamics* software again following step 1 of the installation instructions in Chapter 1. You may want to do so if you have made errors that are too difficult to correct or if you believe that you do not understand the material in the chapter.

If you install the *Dynamics* software again, all previous *Dynamics* software and related data files are overwritten. Assuming that you backed up the data files for Chapters 3 and 4, you can restore your data files for one or both of the chapters by following the instructions in Chapter 1.

Exploring The World Online, Inc.

If you are not already working in Dynamics, open the Dynamics program.

Open The World Online, Inc.

Next, you will explore how The World Online, Inc. (TWO Inc.) uses *Dynamics* in the following areas:

- General Ledger/Financial Statements
- Sales/Customers
- Vendors/Purchasing
- Inventory
- Payroll

While working in this chapter, you will notice that the *Dynamics* palettes for TWO Inc. have more options than the palettes used in earlier chapters for Jackson Supply Company and Waren Distributing. *Dynamics* allows users to customize the palettes to accommodate the size and complexity of each company. Unnecessary palette options were removed for Jackson Supply Company and Waren Distributing. Because TWO Inc. is larger and more complex than the other two companies, all palette options are shown.

General Ledger/Financial Statements

Follow the instructions on pages 134-139 of the Reference book to view the 5/31/98 Balance Sheet on the screen. Be sure to change the Dynamics current date to 5/31/98 before requesting the report. Due to the large size of the report, it may take several seconds to generate it.

Notice that the balance sheet is several pages long. On the first page, there are eleven cash accounts and thirteen accounts receivable accounts.

Use the scroll bar and scrolling arrows to move up and down the balance sheet. When you are done reviewing the balance sheet, close the Screen Output window and then close the Financial Statement Report window.

Sales/Customers

Large companies often have many different types of customers. *Dynamics* allows you to set up several different customer classes, each containing default information specific to the class.

When setting up a new customer in *Dynamics*, you can choose the customer class the new customer belongs to and default information from the class automatically enters the customer record. Next, you will review the customer classes used by TWO Inc.

▣ *Click Setup → Sales → Customer Class to open the Customer Class Setup window.*

▣ *Click once on the Class ID lookup button to open the Customer Classes window.* Notice that TWO Inc. has nine different customer classes covering Australia, Canada, New Zealand, and various states within the United States.

▣ *Close the Customer Classes window and then close the Customer Class Setup window.*

▣ *Click Cards → Sales → Customer to open the Customer Maintenance window.*

▣ *Click once on the Customer ID lookup button to open the Customers and Prospects window. Use the scroll bar and scrolling arrows to view the large number of customers TWO Inc. has set up in the system. When you are done, click the Redisplay button to move to the top of the customer list.*

Next, you will explore one of TWO Inc.'s customer records.

▣ *While still in the Customers and Prospects window, select customer ID ADVANCED0002, Advanced Tech Satellite System to open the Customer Maintenance window for this customer.* Notice that this customer is located in Toronto, Canada.

The Tax Schedule ID box is located in the middle right portion of the window and is used to indicate what taxes should be charged to the customer when a sale is made.

▣ *Zoom on the Tax Schedule ID description field (do not click the lookup button, but rather, zoom on the description field).*

The Tax Schedule Maintenance window for the Canadian sales tax, GST, opens. Because *Dynamics* is designed to work in a multinational environment, the program has the capability of calculating several different foreign taxes for sales and purchases.

▣ *Close the Tax Schedule Maintenance window to return to the Customer Maintenance window for Advanced Tech Satellite System.*

▣ *Click the Options button in the lower right corner to open the Customer Maintenance Options window for the selected customer.*

Notice that the symbol "Z-C$" is in the Currency ID box in the lower right portion of the window. To find out what this symbol means, do the following:

- *Zoom on the Currency ID description field to open the Currency Setup window.* The Description box tells you that the symbol stands for Canadian dollars.

- *Click the Currency ID lookup button (do not zoom on the description field) to open the Currencies window. Click the Redisplay button and notice that the program is capable of handling eight different foreign currencies.*

- *Close all windows to return to the Dynamics main window.*

Vendors/Purchasing

Dynamics is also able to accommodate many different types of vendors. TWO Inc. has ten vendor classes and over 100 vendors in total. TWO Inc. has vendors in Australia, New Zealand, Canada, and various parts of the United States.

- *Follow the instructions on pages 134-139 of the Reference book to view the Accounts Payable Aged Trial Balance report on the screen. Use the scroll bar to move to the last page of the report.* The last line of the Aged Trial Balance report shows that TWO Inc. currently owes 106 vendors over $1.4 million dollars.

- *Close all windows to return to the Dynamics main window.*

Inventory

Dynamics is also able to accommodate a large number and variety of inventory items. TWO Inc. has more than fifty inventory items held at three different sites, but *Dynamics* often deals with a much larger number for many users.

- *Click Cards → Inventory → Item to open the Item Maintenance window.*
- *Use the Item Number lookup button to select item number HDWR-SRG-0001, a Surge Protector.*
- *Click the Pricing button at the bottom of the window to open the Item Pricing Maintenance window for the surge protector.*

Look in the bottom right portion of the window and notice that there are two prices for the surge protector. The first price, $39.95, is for a single unit. The second price, $379.95, is for a case of ten. When entering a sales invoice for TWO Inc., you can sell the surge protectors in either individual units or in cases.

- *Close all windows to return to the Dynamics main window.*

Payroll

Jackson Supply Company and Waren Distributing, Inc. each have only three employees. TWO Inc. has twenty-seven employees in six company departments.

⌨ *Click Reports ➔ Payroll-USA ➔ Wage and Hour to open the Wage and Hour Reports - USA window.* The default selection in the Reports box is the Department Wage and Hour Report.

⌨ *Follow steps B-F in the quick reference table on page 134 of the Reference book to view the Department Wage and Hour Report on the screen.* Notice that the report is organized by the following six company departments: Accounting, Administration, Installation, Purchasing/ Receiving, Sales, and Support Services. TWO Inc. has separate general ledger accounts for each department's payroll-related accounts.

⌨ *Close all windows and return to the Dynamics main window.*

Jackson Supply Company and Waren Distributing, Inc. have no employee deductions except withholdings for federal income tax and F.I.C.A.. In addition to tax withholdings, TWO Inc. has many other payroll deductions.

⌨ *Click Cards ➔ Payroll-USA ➔ Deduction to open the Employee Deduction Maintenance - USA window.*

⌨ *Click once on the Deduction Code lookup button in the top left portion of the window.* Notice that TWO Inc. has seven payroll deduction types.

⌨ *Close all windows to return to the Dynamics main window.*

Recording Sample Transactions for The World Online, Inc.

Next, you will record a few transactions for TWO Inc. to help illustrate the differences between using *Dynamics* for a small company and one that is larger and more complex. You will record the following transactions:

- Make a credit sale with a sales commission
- Purchase goods and services without a purchase order, involving foreign currency
- Pay an employee a bonus check
- Transfer inventory from one site to another
- Post transactions to the general ledger and print a Profit and Loss report

Make a Credit Sale with a Sales Commission

⌨ *Follow the instructions on pages 4-10 of the Reference book to record the following credit sale in Dynamics, but do not post the invoice yet.*

- **Invoice number**: IVC21
- **Date**: June 2, 1998
- **Default Site**: WAREHOUSE
- **Customer Name**: Boyle's Country Inn's
- **Customer ID**: BOYLESCO0001
- **Customer PO #**: RY78341
- **Items sold**:

Item #	Qty.	Unit Price	Description	Unit Cost	Mark-down%
ACCS-RST-DXBK	5	$9.95	Shoulder Rest-Deluxe Black	$4.55	None
ANSW-ATT-1000	10	119.95	AT&T Answering System 1000	$59.29	None

- **General ledger account information**: All default account numbers are correct.

⌨ *Click the Commissions button in the bottom right corner to open the Invoice Commission Entry window.*

⌨ *Click the Show button to reveal details of the sales commission calculation for the invoice.* The default commission calculation is 3%.

⌨ *Zoom on the Salesperson ID description field to open the Salesperson Maintenance window for Ian M. Marsh.* He is the default salesperson assigned to the Boyle's Country Inn's customer record.

Look in the bottom portion of the Salesperson Maintenance window. This part of the window shows year-to-date information for total commissions, commissioned sales, non-commissioned sales, and cost of sales for Mr. Marsh.

⌨ *Close the Salesperson Maintenance window, but do not close the Invoice Commission Entry window yet.*

Assume that for this sale only, Mr. Harsh's commission is 3.5%, not 3%.

⌨ *Change the amount in the Commission Percent box to 3.5%. The new commission amount is $43.72.*

⌨ *Click the OK button to return to the Invoice Entry window. The invoice total should be $1,499.10. If your total is not correct, correct any errors before posting the invoice.*

⌨ *Post the invoice and close the Invoice Entry window.*

Purchase Goods or Services Without a Purchase Order, Involving Foreign Currency

On June 7, 1998, the company received an invoice from the Canadian location of International TeleCom Associates. TWO Inc. issued a check on the same day in full payment of the invoice.

⌨ *Follow the instructions on pages 68-73 in the Reference book to record the invoice and payment using the following information, but do not close the Payables Transaction Entry Distribution window yet (complete only steps A through J on page 68 of the Reference book).*

- **Description**: Installation charges
- **PO Number**: None
- **Vendor Name**: International TeleCom Assoc.
- **Vendor ID**: INTERNAT0001 (be sure to select the Canadian location, *not INTERNAT0002*, the Australian location)
- **Payment Terms**: Net 30
- **Currency ID**: Z-C$ (Canadian dollars)
- **Vendor's invoice number**: 1008
- **Shipping method**: MAIL
- **Tax Schedule ID**: COMPANYPUR
- **Amount of invoice**: C$1,500.00 (1,500 Canadian dollars)*
- **Payment information**:
     Ck. number: #20008
     Bank: First National
     Check amount: C$1,500.00 (1,500 Canadian dollars)*

- **General ledger account information**: All default account numbers are correct.

* *The "C" appears before the "$" to indicate Canadian dollars.*

After clicking on the Distributions button, notice that *Dynamics* automatically calculates the foreign currency translation from Canadian dollars to US dollars. The Debit and Credit boxes in the scrolling window of the Payables Transaction Entry Distribution window contain the US dollar amount ($1,080.75), while the Originating Debit and Originating Credit boxes contain the Canadian dollar amount (C$1,500.00).

If the amounts on your screen agree with the amounts above, click the OK button to return to the Payables Transaction Entry window. Post the transaction and close the Payables Transaction Entry window. If there are errors, correct them before posting.

Pay an Employee a Bonus Check

Follow the instructions on pages 74-79 of the Reference book to record a bonus check to an employee, using the information that follows. After you record the transaction, close the Payroll Manual Check - Adjustment Entry - USA window.

- **Checkbook ID**: PAYROLL
- **Check number**: 10054
- **Check date and posted date**: June 15, 1998
- **Employee Name**: Toshi Y. Minami
- **Employee ID**: MINA0001
- **Pay period**: 6-15-98 to 6-15-98
- **Bonus amount (Code = BONS)**: $2,000.00
- **Federal income tax withholding (Transaction Type = Federal Tax)**: $400.00
- **Other withholdings**: None
- **Net bonus check (check amount)**: $1,600.00

Transfer Inventory from One Site to Another

As discussed earlier in the chapter, TWO Inc. has three sites where inventory is held. Like other companies with inventory at multiple locations, TWO Inc. transfers inventory from one site to another as needed. Next, you will use the Item Transfer Entry window to record an inventory transfer transaction. Because you have not used this window in Chapters 2 through 4, detailed instructions are provided to record the transfer. Information necessary to record the transfer is shown in the following box.

- **Date of transfer**: June 20, 1998
- **Default Site ID information**:
  From: WAREHOUSE (Main Site)
  To: NORTH (North Store)

- **Items transferred**:

Item #	Qty.	Description	From Site	To Site
ANSW-PAN-2460	10	Panasonic KX-T2460	WAREHOUSE	NORTH
PHON-ATT-53BK	5	Cordless-AT&T 53 BK-Black	WAREHOUSE	NORTH

- **General ledger account information**: All default account numbers are correct.

📠 *Click Transactions → Inventory → Transfer Entry (not Transaction Entry) to open the Item Transfer Entry window.*

📠 *Type the transfer date in the Date box.*

The From and To boxes in the Default Site ID area of the window (top right portion of the window) are used to indicate where the inventory is being transferred from and where it is being transferred to.

📠 *Use the From lookup button to select WAREHOUSE.*

📠 *Use the To lookup button to select NORTH.*

📠 *Use the Item Number lookup button to select the first inventory item being transferred.*

📠 *Type the quantity transferred in the Quantity box.*

📠 *Move through the From Site and To Site boxes to reach the next blank Item Number box.*

📠 *Repeat the three preceding steps for the second item.*

📠 *Review the Item Transfer Entry window for completeness and accuracy. If there are errors correct them before going to the next step.*

📠 *Click the Post button and close the Item Transfer Entry window.*

To verify that the preceding transfer entry is properly recorded in *Dynamics*, complete the following steps:

- *Click Inquiry → Inventory → Transaction to open the Inventory Transaction Inquiry window.*
- *Select Transfer in the Document Type box.*
- *Use the Number lookup button to select the transfer entry previously prepared (there will be only one entry to choose from).*
- *Click the Show button to reveal all lines in the scrolling window.*
- *Notice that the transfer entry you recorded is reflected in the window.*
- *Close the Inventory Transaction Inquiry window.*

Post Transactions to the General Ledger and Print a Profit and Loss Report

Next, you will post the transactions you just recorded plus other unposted transactions to TWO Inc.'s general ledger and print a profit and loss report through June 30, 1998.

- *Follow the instructions on pages 124-127 of the Reference book to post the transactions to the general ledger. When all entries are posted, close the Series Posting window.*
- *Follow the instructions on pages 134-139 of the Reference book to print a hard copy of the Profit and Loss report through June 30, 1998 (called a Statement of Income and Retained Earnings on the Reference Summary Card). Remember to change the current date to June 30, 1998 before requesting the report.*

Compare selected items off your printed Profit and Loss report to the check figures provided on page 5-12. If any amounts are different, return to the transactions you processed for TWO Inc. earlier and make the necessary corrections. See Appendix A in the Reference book for error correction instructions. Remember that another option (which may be quicker and easier for you) is to reload the *Dynamics* software and redo the TWO Inc. transactions. When all errors are corrected, print a corrected Profit and Loss report to turn in to your instructor.

- *After printing the report correctly, close all windows to return to the Dynamics main window.*

After you print a hard copy of the Profit and Loss report, hand it in to your instructor. All procedures are now complete for this chapter.

The World Online, Inc.
Profit and Loss Check Figures
For 1/1/98 to 6/30/98

	Current Period	**Current YTD**
Gross Sales	$ 1,249.25	$1,798,834.48
Net Sales	1,249.25	1,741,952.69
Total Cost of Goods Sold	615.65	603,668.31
Gross Profit on Sales	633.60	1,138,284.38
Total Administrative Expense	1,080.75	640,361.04
Total Salaries Expense	2,043.72	121,784.85
Total Operating Expenses	3,124.47	799,612.52
Net Profit on Sales	(2,490.87)	338,671.86
Net Income Before Taxes	(2,490.87)	338,387.33

Note: No taxes have been accrued for this interim report. Thus, net income will be the same as net income before taxes.

CHAPTER 6

New Company Setup

Introduction

In this chapter you will set up a new company in *Dynamics*. Office Furniture Plus is an office furniture retailer that has been in operation for five years. The company has maintained a manual accounting system since its inception. Due to a significant increase in sales volume, the company's management has decided to change to a computerized system using *Dynamics* as of January 1, 1999.

If, at any time, you decide that you want to start the chapter over, you may do so by installing the *Dynamics* software again following Step 1 of the installation instructions in Chapter 1. You may want to do so if you have made errors that are too difficult to correct or if you believe that you do not understand the material in this chapter. If you do this, you will almost certainly want to back up your data files for Chapters 3 and 4, then restore them after you have reinstalled the *Dynamics* software. See Chapter 1 for instructions.

Certain *Dynamics* procedures for setting up a new company are quite time-consuming. Most of these procedures relate to general system setup and have already been completed for Office Furniture Plus to reduce your time on the assignment. Also, for a typical company using *Dynamics*, there are a large number of general ledger accounts, customers, vendors, inventory items, and employees. It is necessary to enter information about each of these, including beginning balances. To minimize time requirements, the number of general ledger accounts, customers, vendors, inventory items, and employees is kept extremely small.

The procedures you will perform in this chapter include:

- Modify the default chart of accounts
- Enter general ledger beginning balances
- Set up a customer class and add customer records
- Enter customer beginning balances
- Add vendor records
- Add inventory item records
- Enter inventory item beginning quantities
- Add employee records
- Print a beginning trial balance
- Record transactions for the new company
- Post transactions to the general ledger and print a trial balance

Each of these procedures is described in a section that follows.

Modify the Default Chart of Accounts

When setting up a new company in *Dynamics,* a user can either enter the company's chart of accounts manually or choose a default chart of accounts from a list of thirteen different industry types and three different business types (corporation, partnership, and sole proprietorship). *Dynamics* includes a default chart of accounts for a retail store operating as a corporation, which was selected for Office Furniture plus and has already been included as part of general system setup. You will modify the default chart of accounts so it matches the one used in the company's manual accounting system.

- *If you are not already working in Dynamics, open the Dynamics program.*
- *Open Office Furniture Plus.*
- *Click Cards → Financial → Account to open the Account Maintenance window.*
- *Click the lookup button next to the Account box. This opens the Accounts window, where you can view all existing general ledger accounts for the company.*
- *Use the scroll bar and the up and down scroll arrows to review the company's chart of accounts. When you are done reviewing, close the Accounts window to return to the Account Maintenance window.*

To match the chart of accounts Office Furniture Plus uses in its manual accounting system, certain changes are necessary. You will use the Account Maintenance window to make these changes. The following general ledger accounts are to be added:

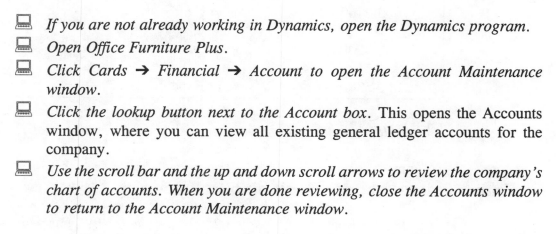

Account #	Description	Category	Posting Type	Typical Balance
000-1110-00	Cash - Savings	Cash	Balance Sheet	Debit
000-1250-00	Allowance for Uncollectible Accounts	Accts. Rec.	Balance Sheet	Credit
000-5230-00	Van Repairs & Maintenance	Administrative Expense	Profit & Loss	Debit
000-5400-00	Bad Debt Expense	Bad Debt Expense	Profit & Loss	Debit

📖 *Follow the instructions on page 112 of the Reference book to add the four preceding general ledger accounts.*

Next, you will delete the following accounts from the default chart of accounts which management has decided not to use:

Account #	Description
000-2110-00	Discounts Available
000-2160-00	Leases Payable
000-3200-00	Preferred Stock
000-5300-00	Warranty Expense

📖 *Follow the instructions on page 114 of the Reference book to delete the four preceding general ledger accounts.*

Enter General Ledger Beginning Balances

The trial balance on page 6-21 shows the 1-1-99 general ledger beginning balances for Office Furniture Plus. Because the company is starting to use *Dynamics* at the beginning of the year, all income statement account balances are zero.

You will use the Transaction Entry window to record the company's general ledger beginning balances in *Dynamics*. Enter all account balances using one general journal entry.

📖 *Prepare a 1-1-99 general journal entry in Dynamics to record the company's general ledger beginning balances. Follow the instructions on pages 80-84 of the Reference book to prepare the entry.*

Observe that after you enter the account number and press [Return], the cursor automatically moves to the debit or credit column that is typical for this account. Recall in the previous assignment that you entered Debit or Credit for "Typical Balance" each time a general ledger account is added. This is a good example of the use of default information.

Set Up a Customer Class and Add Customer Records

Entering customer records for a new company can be a time-consuming process. There are three separate processes, each of which you will do in this section:

- Set up a customer class
- Add customer records for each customer into the system
- Enter customer beginning balances and related information into the customer records. The total of all customers' beginning balances must equal the general ledger balance that you entered in the previous assignment.

Set Up a Customer Class

Dynamics allows users to set up a *customer class* for groups of customers with similar characteristics. Once a customer class is created, this class can be selected when setting up a new customer record in *Dynamics*. Default information from the class is automatically added to the new customer record and can then be modified for the individual customer. Customer classes also make it easier to make global changes to groups of customers at once without having to enter the changes into each customer's record. For example, if a company changes the finance charge percentage for all customers in a class, this change can be entered once in the customer class record and "rolled down" to each customer in the class.

In the first part of this section, you will set up a customer class for Office Furniture Plus's local business customers.

🖳 *Click Setup → Sales → Customer Class to open the Customer Class Setup window.*

🖳 *Enter the following information in the Customer Class Setup window, but do not click the Save button yet. Use the Lookup button for payment terms and shipping method.*

Note: If a box in the window is not mentioned below, no entry is necessary.

- **Class ID**: LOCAL
- **Description**: Local business customers
- **Balance Type**: Open Item
- **Finance Charge**: None
- **Minimum Payment**: No Minimum
- **Credit Limit**: $15,000
- **Writeoff**: Maximum $500
- **Payment Terms**: 2/10, Net 30
- **Shipping Method**: LOCAL DELIVERY
- **Tax Schedule ID**: SALE
- **Price Level**: RETAIL

After you enter all information in the main window, you are ready to enter the default general ledger account information for the class.

⌨ *Click the Accounts button in the lower right corner to open the Customer Class Accounts Setup window.*

⌨ *Select HOLLAND (Holland Savings Bank) in the Checkbook ID box which the authors entered as default information earlier as a part of preliminary setup.*

⌨ *Enter the following general ledger account information by using the Lookup button beside each account:*

Box Description	Account #	Account Description
Accounts Receivable	000-1200-00	Accounts Receivable
Sales	000-4100-00	Sales
Cost of Sales	000-4500-00	Cost of Goods Sold
Inventory	000-1300-00	Inventory
Terms Discount Taken	000-4400-00	Sales Discounts
Terms Discount Available	N/A	N/A
Finance Charges	N/A	N/A
Writeoffs	000-1250-00	Allowance for Uncollectible Accounts

⌨ *After all general ledger accounts are entered, click the OK button to return to the Customer Class Setup window.*

⌨ *Click the Save button to save the customer class record.*

⌨ *Although each Lookup button contains many options, observe that the default information you have entered comes up automatically when the class is selected.*

⌨ *Close the Customer Class Setup window.*

Add Customer Records

After you create the customer class, you are ready to add customer records for this class. Although Office Furniture Plus has many customers in the LOCAL class, you will enter only two customer records. Information for each of the two customers follows. *Note that all default information from the LOCAL class is correct for each customer unless otherwise noted.*

⌨ *Follow the instructions on page 104 of the Reference book to add the first customer record below.*

```
                            First Customer
  ●   Customer ID: 1001
  ●   Name: Dickerson & May P.C.
  ●   Class ID: LOCAL
  ●   Address ID: PRIMARY
  ●   Contact: James M. Dickerson
  ●   Address: 600 Capital Ave. Suite 602, Holland, MI 49024
  ●   Phone #: 616-555-7800
  ●   Fax #: 616-555-8889
  ●   Shipping Method: UPS Red
  ●   Credit Limit: $10,000 (click the Options button to enter the Customer
      Maintenance Options window and change the credit limit)
```

⌨ *Follow the instructions on page 104 of the Reference book to add the second customer record below.*

<table>
<tr><td colspan="2" align="center">Second Customer</td></tr>
<tr><td>●</td><td>Customer ID: 1002</td></tr>
<tr><td>●</td><td>Name: Metzgar Insurance Company</td></tr>
<tr><td>●</td><td>Class ID: LOCAL</td></tr>
<tr><td>●</td><td>Address ID: PRIMARY</td></tr>
<tr><td>●</td><td>Contact: Marilyn Metzgar</td></tr>
<tr><td>●</td><td>Address: 8900 Wellston Blvd., Grand Haven, MI 49417</td></tr>
<tr><td>●</td><td>Phone #: 616-555-0002</td></tr>
<tr><td>●</td><td>Fax #: 616-555-5231</td></tr>
<tr><td>●</td><td>Payment Terms: Net 30</td></tr>
</table>

After clicking the Save button to add the second customer, complete the following step to review the customers you have added.

💻 *Click the Customer ID Lookup button and observe that there are two customers included.*

Enter Customer Beginning Balances and Related Information

The next step in setting up customers in *Dynamics* is to enter customer beginning balances. Although you already entered the total accounts receivable balance when entering general ledger beginning balances, you must enter individual customer balances receivable into the *Dynamics* Sales module. To avoid double-posting the beginning balances to the general ledger, you must first turn off general ledger posting from the Sales module.

💻 *Click Setup → Posting → Posting to open the Posting Setup window.*
💻 *Select Sales in the Series box.*
💻 *Select Receivables Sales Entry in the Origin list box.*
💻 *Click the check box next to the words "Post to General Ledger" to remove the check mark.* The check box is located below the Series box.
💻 *Click the Save button and close the Posting Setup window.*

After general ledger posting is turned off, you can enter the customer beginning balances using the Receivables Transaction Entry window. The reason for entering the sales transaction is to input all information into *Dynamics* related to the accounts receivable. The Receivables Transaction Entry window is used now instead of the Invoice Entry window because no inventory items have been set up yet for Office Furniture Plus. Recall from previous chapters that a credit sale is entered in the Invoice Entry window by entering specific inventory items and quantities sold to a customer.

Assume that the company's entire accounts receivable balance is due from one customer, Metzgar Insurance Company, customer ID #1002. A credit sale was made to the customer on December 28, 1998. Other details of the sale follow:

- **Document Type**: Sales/Invoices
- **Number**: 2402 (invoice number)
- **Description**: Credit sale
- **Document Date**: December 28, 1998
- **Cost**: $9,513.00
- **Sales**: $14,000.00
- **Taxes**: $840.00
- **Invoice total**: $14,840.00
- **All default general ledger accounts are correct.**

🖥 *Click Transactions → Sales → Transaction Entry to open the Receivables Transaction Entry window.*

🖥 *Type* [2402] *in the Number box.*

🖥 *Type* [Credit sale] *in the Description box.*

🖥 *Type* [122898] *in the Document Date box.*

🖥 *Select* 1002 (Metzgar Insurance Company) *in the Customer ID box.*

🖥 *Type* [9513.00] *in the Cost box.*

🖥 *Type* [14000.00] *in the Sales box.*

🖥 *Click the Tax box. Note: do not click on the adjacent expansion button, but click on the Tax box itself.* Notice that *Dynamics* automatically calculates the $840.00 sales tax.

If the Tax box is blank, review the contents of the Tax Schedule ID box. If the Tax Schedule ID box is blank, you probably forgot to enter the default Tax Schedule ID when setting up the LOCAL customer class on pages 6-5 to 6-7. If you need to correct the LOCAL customer class information, complete the following eight steps. If the amount in the Tax box is correct, skip the following eight steps and continue entering information for invoice #2402.

1. 🖳 *Click the Delete button and click Delete again when asked if you want to delete this document.*

2. 🖳 *Close the Receivables Transaction Entry window.*

3. 🖳 *Click Setup → Sales → Customer Class to open the Customer Class Setup window.*

4. 🖳 *Use the Class ID lookup button to select LOCAL.*

5. 🖳 *Use the Tax Schedule ID lookup button to select SALE.*

6. 🖳 *Click the Save button and click Yes when asked if you want to roll down changes to customers in this class.* This allows you to make the change only once and have it correct all customers in the class.

7. 🖳 *Close the Customer Class Setup window.*

8. 🖳 *Follow the steps on page 6-9 to re-enter information for invoice #2402. After the amount in the Tax box is correct, complete the steps that follow to finish entering information for invoice #2402.*

🖳 *Review the amount in the Total box. If the total is $14,840.00, click the Post button to post the transaction to the Sales module. If there are errors, correct them before posting.*

🖳 *After the beginning balance transaction is posted, close the Receivables Transaction Entry window.*

The final step after entering customer beginning balances is to return to the Posting Setup window and reactivate general ledger posting.

🖳 *Click Setup → Posting → Posting to open the Posting Setup window.*

🖳 *Select Sales in the Series box.*

🖳 *Select Receivables Sales Entry in the Origin list box.*

🖳 *Click the check box next to the words "Post to General Ledger" to reinstate the check mark.*

🖳 *Click the Save button and close the Posting Setup window.*

Add Vendor Records

Vendor setup procedures in *Dynamics* are similar to customer setup procedures using processes almost identical to the three that you have just completed. You can create a vendor class for vendors with similar characteristics and then load default information from the class into each new vendor record. For this section, you will add two of Office Furniture Plus's vendors using default information from a vendor class that has already been created for the company. *Note that all default information from the vendor class is correct for each vendor unless otherwise noted.*

💻 *Follow the instructions on page 108 of the Reference book to add the first vendor record below.*

First Vendor

- **Vendor ID**: OAK
- **Name**: The Oak Factory
- **Class ID**: TRADE
- **Address ID**: PRIMARY
- **Contact**: Ronald McPherson
- **Address**: 566 Chilson Ave. Romeo, MI 48065
- **Phone #**: 810-555-1200
- **Fax #**: 810-555-5227
- **Tax Schedule ID**: Leave blank
- **Shipping Method**: UPS Blue
- **Vendor Account**: 54678
- **All default general ledger accounts are correct**.

💻 *Follow the instructions on page 108 of the Reference book to add the following second vendor record.*

```
┌─────────────────────────────────────────────────────────────────┐
│                         Second Vendor                           │
│  ●  Vendor ID: AVON                                              │
│  ●  Name: Avondale Properties                                   │
│  ●  Class ID: TRADE                                             │
│  ●  Address ID: PRIMARY                                         │
│  ●  Contact: Christina Wright                                   │
│  ●  Address: 15700 West Huron St., Otsego, MI 49078             │
│  ●  Phone #: 616-555-5784                                       │
│  ●  Fax #: None                                                 │
│  ●  Tax Schedule ID: Leave blank                               │
│  ●  Shipping Method: Blank                                      │
│  ●  Vendor Account: 15445                                       │
│  ●  Payment Terms: Check (Use Vendor Maintenance Options window to│
│     enter)                                                      │
│  ●  General ledger account distributions: Correct except that the│
│     Purchases account should be #000-5260-00, Rent Expense.    │
└─────────────────────────────────────────────────────────────────┘
```

The final step in setting up vendors in *Dynamics* is to enter the beginning balances due to vendors. The process is similar to entering beginning balances receivable from customers, except that the Payables Transaction Entry window is used. Because the procedures are somewhat time-consuming and are similar to those you performed in the previous section, you will not do vendor beginning balance procedures. Recall that the company's beginning accounts payable balance is zero.

Add Inventory Item Records

As you have seen in other chapters, *Dynamics* uses a perpetual inventory system. When the conversion from the manual system to *Dynamics* occurs, each inventory item on hand must be added to the Inventory module before any transactions can be recorded. In this section, you will add three of Office Furniture Plus's inventory items using default information from an item class that has already been created for Office Furniture Plus.

Like customer classes for accounts receivable, the Inventory module permits the use of inventory classes to make it easier to enter inventory items. Because you have already practiced setting up a customer class, and setting up an inventory class is similar, default information has already been entered for an inventory class to reduce your time. *Note that all default information from the class is correct for each inventory item unless otherwise noted.*

💻 *Follow the instructions on page 120 of the Reference book for Inventory Item Maintenance to add the first inventory item record below. **Be sure to click Yes when asked if you want to update the item with information from the FURN class**.*

First Inventory Item
- **Item Number**: 101
- **Description**: Basic desk
- **Class ID**: FURN
- **Current Cost**: $223.00
- **List Price**: $330.00
- **Site ID assigned**: MAIN (Warehouse)
- **Vendor ID assigned**: OAK (The Oak Factory)
- **Vendor Item**: 456781

💻 *Follow the instructions on page 120 of the Reference book for Item Maintenance to add the second inventory item record below. **Be sure to click Yes when asked if you want to update the item with information from the FURN class**.*

Second Inventory Item
- **Item Number**: 102
- **Description**: Desk chair
- **Class ID**: FURN
- **Current Cost**: $122.00
- **List Price**: $175.00
- **Site ID assigned**: MAIN (Warehouse)
- **Vendor ID assigned**: OAK (The Oak Factory)
- **Vendor Item**: 642175

💻 *Follow the instructions on page 120 of the Reference book for Item Maintenance to add the third inventory item record below. **Be sure to click Yes when asked if you want to update the item with information from the FURN class**.*

```
┌─────────────────────────────────────────────────────────┐
│                   Third Inventory Item                  │
│   ●  Item Number: 103                                   │
│   ●  Description: Desk lamp                             │
│   ●  Class ID: FURN                                     │
│   ●  Current Cost: $28.00                              │
│   ●  List Price: $42.00                                │
│   ●  Site ID assigned: MAIN (Warehouse)               │
│   ●  Vendor ID assigned: OAK (The Oak Factory)        │
│   ●  Vendor Item: 784120                               │
└─────────────────────────────────────────────────────────┘
```

Enter Inventory Item Beginning Quantities

After all inventory item records are added, beginning quantities must be entered for each item. Similar to entering customer and vendor beginning balances, the first step is to turn off general ledger posting so that the beginning quantity entry will not cause double-posting of the beginning inventory's cost to the general ledger.

⌨ *Click Setup → Posting → Posting to open the Posting Setup window.*

⌨ *Select Inventory in the Series box.*

⌨ *Select Transaction Entry in the Origin list box.*

⌨ *Click the check box next to the words "Post to General Ledger" to remove the check mark.*

⌨ *Click the Save button and close the Posting Setup window.*

Beginning inventory quantities are entered through the Item Transaction Entry window as an adjustment transaction. All quantities are entered in one transaction window. Assume that the company's inventory on hand consists solely of the three inventory items you added in the last section.

⌨ *Follow the instructions on pages 86-90 of the Reference book (Adjust Perpetual Inventory Records) to enter the beginning inventory quantities below at 1-1-99. Although the reference section covers adjustment of inventory quantities to a physical count, the procedures are the same for entering beginning inventory quantities. The quantity adjustment for each item is the beginning quantity.*

Item #	Description	Beginning Quantity
101	Basic desk	172
102	Desk chair	225
103	Desk lamp	312

After you enter the beginning quantities, you must reactivate general ledger posting from the Inventory module.

- *Click Setup → Posting → Posting to open the Posting Setup window.*
- *Select Inventory in the Series box.*
- *Select Transaction Entry in the Origin list box.*
- *Click the check box next to the words "Post to General Ledger" to reinstate the check mark.*
- *Click the Save button and close the Posting Setup window.*

Add Employee Records

The Payroll module is the final module for which *Dynamics* setup procedures are necessary. In this section, you will add two of Office Furniture Plus's employees using default information from two employee classes that have already been created for the company. One employee is an hourly employee and the other is a salaried employee. Again, the classes information has already been entered in the system to reduce your time. *Note that all default information from the employee classes is correct unless otherwise noted.*

- *Follow the instructions on page 116 of the Reference book for adding an employee record to add the following first employee record.*

First Employee - Hourly

- **Employee ID**: ASHF0001
- **Class ID**: HOUR
- **Name**: Kevin Ashford
- **Social Security #**: 549-56-3982
- **Department**: WARE (Warehouse)
- **Job Title**: STOCK (Warehouse stock employee)
- **Address**: 462 Sibley Lane, Holland, MI 49024
- **Phone #**: 616-555-8888
- **Start Date**: 6-22-97
- **Birth Date**: 3-19-60
- **Ethnic Origin**: Black

Tax Information:
- **Federal Filing Status**: Married
- **Federal Exemptions**: 4

Pay Code Information:
- **Hourly rate**: $7.00
- **Overtime rate**: $10.50

💻 *Follow the instructions on page 116 of the Reference book for adding an employee record to add the following second employee record.*

Second Employee - Salaried

- **Employee ID**: TROX0001
- **Class ID**: SALARY
- **Name**: Sharon Troxel
- **Social Security #**: 642-55-1342
- **Department**: ACCT (Accounting)
- **Job Title**: CONT (Controller)
- **Address**: 185 Post Ave., Zeeland, MI 49464
- **Phone #**: 616-555-0052
- **Start Date**: 4-30-96
- **Birth Date**: 7-22-65
- **Ethnic Origin**: Caucasian

Tax Information:
- **Federal Filing Status**: Single
- **Federal Exemptions**: 2

Pay Code Information:
- **Salary**: $900.00 per week

Print a Beginning Trial Balance

Print a hard copy of the general ledger trial balance (quick summary trial balance) for Office Furniture Plus, using the Reference book instructions on pages 134-139.

The balances in the printed trial balance should match those on page 6-21. If there are errors, correct them by recording the appropriate general journal entry. When all balances are correct, go to the next section where you will record a sample set of transactions for Office Furniture Plus.

Process Transactions and Do Other Activities for the New Company

In this section, you will process transactions for Office Furniture Plus for the first week of January 1999 using *Dynamics*. You will process transactions and do other activities.

In processing these transactions or doing other activities, you should first find the appropriate reference pages by using the Reference Summary Card and then use the Reference book to guide you.

Transaction #1

📖 *Record the following transaction using Dynamics.*

On January 2, 1999, the company sold merchandise on account to Dickerson & May P.C. Other details of the credit sale follow:

- **Invoice number**: 2403
- **Date**: January 2, 1999
- **Default Site**: MAIN (Warehouse)
- **Customer Name**: Dickerson & May P.C.
- **Customer ID**: 1001
- **Customer PO #**: 89458
- **Items sold**:

Item #	Qty.	Unit Price	Description	Unit Cost	Mkdown %
102	5	$175.00	Desk chair	$122.00	None
103	10	$ 42.00	Desk lamp	$ 28.00	None

- **General ledger account information**: All default account numbers are correct.
- **Invoice total** (check figure): $1,372.70, including tax

Transaction #2

📖 *Record the following transaction using Dynamics.*

On January 3, 1999, the company received a check from Metzgar Insurance Company in full payment of an accounts receivable for invoice #2402. Other details of the collection follow:

- **Amount received**: $14,840.00 (no discount; terms were Net 30)
- **Customer's check #**: 10053
- **General ledger account information**: All default accounts numbers are correct.

Transaction #3

⌨ *Process the following purchase order using Dynamics.*

On January 3, 1999, the company ordered inventory from The Oak Factory. The inventory was not received on January 3. Other details of the purchase order follow:

- **PO Number**: 1407
- **Date**: January 3, 1999
- **Default Site**: MAIN (Warehouse)
- **Vendor Name**: The Oak Factory
- **Vendor ID**: OAK
- **Inventory items ordered**:

Item #	Quantity Ordered	Unit Cost	Description
101	50	$223.00	Basic desk
102	35	$122.00	Desk chair

- **Purchase order total** (check figure): $15,420.00

Transaction #4

⌨ *Record the following receipt of goods in Dynamics.*

On January 5, 1999, Office Furniture Plus received the inventory merchandise from The Oak Factory for purchase order #1407, along with invoice #56781. Other details of the purchase follow:

- **Date goods were received**: January 5, 1999
- **Vendor ID**: OAK (The Oak Factory)
- **Goods shipped/invoiced**: All goods ordered were received
- **No trade discount, freight, miscellaneous charges, or taxes**
- **Payment terms**: Net 30
- **General ledger account information**: All default information is correct.
- **Invoice total (check figure)**: $15,420.00

Transaction #5

⌨ *Record the following cash disbursement* transaction.

On January 7, 1999, the company issued a check to The Oak Factory in full payment of invoice #56781. Other details of the cash disbursement follow:

- **Vendor ID**: OAK
- **Check number #**: 124307
- **Check amount**: $15,420.00 (no discount; terms were Net 30)
- **Invoice paid**: #56781
- **General ledger account information**: All default information is correct

Transaction #6

⌨ *Record Sharon Troxel's weekly pay in Dynamics*. Details are as follows:

- **Check number**: 124308
- **Check date and posting date**: January 8, 1999
- **Employee ID**: TROX0001
- **Pay period**: 1-01-99 to 01-07-99
- **Gross pay (Code = Salary)**: $900.00
- **Federal income tax withholding (Transaction Type = Federal Tax)**: $175.43
- **FICA withholding (Transaction Type = FICA/Soc. Sec. Tax)** : $68.85
- **Net pay (check amount)**: $655.72

Other Activity #1

⌨ *Post the January 1999 transactions to the general ledger.*

Other Activity #2

⌨ *Print a hard copy of the general ledger trial balance (quick summary trial balance) for Office Furniture Plus*. Notice that the January 1999 transactions you recorded are reflected in this trial balance.

Compare the balances on your printed trial balance with those on page 6-22. If there are any differences, make necessary corrections as you have learned in previous chapters. When your balances agree with those on page 6-22, print a corrected trial balance and hand it in to your instructor. All procedures are now complete for this chapter.

Office Furniture Plus
Beginning Trial Balance at 1-1-99

Account #	Description	Balance Dr. (Cr.)
000-1100-00	Cash-Checking	16,875.42
000-1110-00	Cash-Savings	7,852.50
000-1200-00	Accounts Receivable	14,840.00
000-1250-00	Allowance for Uncollectible Accounts	(750.00)
000-1270-00	Investments	6,200.00
000-1300-00	Inventory	74,542.00
000-1410-00	Prepaid Insurance	0.00
000-1420-00	Prepaid Taxes	0.00
000-1510-00	Equipment	16,495.00
000-1515-00	Accumulated Depreciation—Equipment	(7,069.29)
000-1530-00	Autos/Delivery Vans	20,585.00
000-1535-00	Accumulated Depreciation—Autos/Delivery Vans	(8,822.14)
000-2100-00	Accounts Payable	0.00
000-2150-00	Notes Payable—Current	0.00
000-2170-00	Interest Payable	0.00
000-2260-00	FUTA Taxes Payable	(122.74)
000-2265-00	SUTA Taxes Payable	(374.98)
000-2270-00	FICA Taxes Payable	0.00
000-2275-00	Federal Taxes Payable	0.00
000-2290-00	Sales Taxes Payable	(1,248.76)
000-2410-00	Notes Payable—Long-Term	(33,000.00)
000-3000-00	Retained Earnings	(56,002.01)
000-3100-00	Common Stock	(50,000.00)
000-3110-00	Paid-in Capital	0.00

Account	Description	Beginning Balance	Net Change	Ending Balance
000-1100-00	Cash-Checking	$0.00	$15,639.70	$15,639.70
000-1110-00	Cash - Savings	$0.00	$7,852.50	$7,852.50
000-1200-00	Accounts Receivable	$0.00	$1,372.70	$1,372.70
000-1250-00	Allowance for Uncollectible Accounts	$0.00	($750.00)	($750.00)
000-1270-00	Investments	$0.00	$6,200.00	$6,200.00
000-1300-00	Inventory	$0.00	$89,072.00	$89,072.00
000-1510-00	Equipment	$0.00	$16,495.00	$16,495.00
000-1515-00	Accum Depr-Equipment	$0.00	($7,069.29)	($7,069.29)
000-1530-00	Autos/Delivery Vans	$0.00	$20,585.00	$20,585.00
000-1535-00	Accum Depr-Autos/Deliv Vans	$0.00	($8,822.14)	($8,822.14)
000-2100-00	Accounts Payable	$0.00	$0.00	$0.00
000-2260-00	FUTA Taxes Payable	$0.00	($122.74)	($122.74)
000-2265-00	SUTA Taxes Payable	$0.00	($374.98)	($374.98)
000-2270-00	FICA Taxes Payable	$0.00	($137.70)	($137.70)
000-2275-00	Federal Taxes Payable	$0.00	($175.43)	($175.43)
000-2290-00	Sales Taxes Payable	$0.00	($1,326.46)	($1,326.46)
000-2410-00	Notes Payable-Long Term	$0.00	($33,000.00)	($33,000.00)
000-3000-00	Retained Earnings	$0.00	($56,002.01)	($56,002.01)
000-3100-00	Common Stock	$0.00	($50,000.00)	($50,000.00)
000-4100-00	Sales	$0.00	($1,295.00)	($1,295.00)
000-4500-00	Costs of Goods Sold	$0.00	$890.00	$890.00
000-5005-00	Wages and Salaries	$0.00	$900.00	$900.00
000-5160-00	Payroll Tax Expense	$0.00	$68.85	$68.85

Total Accounts: 23

Grand Totals: $0.00 $0.00 $0.00